Papua New Guinea - Its Land and People

SOCIAL SCIENCE PUPIL BOOK

Published by Department of Education Papua New Guinea

First Published 1987
Reprinted 1988, 1992, 1993, 1994, 1995, 1996 (three times), 1997, 1998, 1999 (three times), 2000 (twice), 2002, 2007, 2008 (twice), 2016 (D)

ISBN 9980 58047 X
ISBN 978 9980 58047 4
National Library of Papua New Guinea

Typeset by Syarikat Seng Teik Sdn. Bhd., Malaysia
Printed in Australia by Ligare Pty Ltd.
Published by Department of Education, Papua New Guinea
Prepared by Oxford University Press
253 Normanby Road, South Melbourne, Australia

Acknowledgements

This book was written by Diane Ranck and Peter Bridger. The Papua New Guinea Department of Education acknowledges the contribution of many individuals at the Curriculum Unit and on the Social Science Syllabus Advisory Committee to the trialling and review of the book. The participation of the teachers and students at the trial schools—Mongop, Laloki, Tapini, Kimbe, Goroka, Muaina, Kilakila, Badihagwa, and Gerehu Provincial High Schools—is greatly appreciated.

The textbook development work was co-ordinated by the late Greg Chariton, in the earlier stages, and subsequently by Mike McRory, Senior Curriculum Officer for Social Science at the Curriculum Unit.

The publisher wishes to thank the following people and organisations for supplying, and granting permission to reproduce, photographs:

Bettmann Archive pp. 6, 17; Herald and Weekly Times p. 7; Dale Mann/Retrospect p. 13 (top left); Hec Gallagher p. 14 (top); Department of Agriculture and Rural Affairs, Victoria, p. 21; CSIRO, Australia, pp. 31 (left), 54.

Secretary's Message

The topic **Papua New Guinea—Land and People** is the third term's work in the Grade Seven Provincial High School Social Science Course. It is the first of the four topics which develop the theme **People and Environment** through Grades Seven to Ten.

The book is the core learning material for the topic. A supporting set of teaching notes is available. The teaching notes advise the teachers on how to make the best use of the pupil's book.

The material in the book integrates the presentation of information, the development of ideas, reinforcement and application of Social Science skills and the fostering of attitudes.

Three types of activities appear at the end of each section. There are Exercises to ensure comprehension of the material; there are Things to Discuss and Things to Do. The activities combine work on sections of the book with direct investigations both inside and outside school.

This book is one of the items of instructional material produced for Provincial High Schools in Papua New Guinea as part of the Education III Textbook Sub-Project.

S G ROAKEINA
Secretary for Education

Contents

1. Geography

What is Geography?

In this book we are going to study the **geography** of Papua New Guinea. Geography involves describing the things we see around us—our **environment**. Geographers also study the reasons why the parts of the environment are like they are. They examine the way in which parts of the environment depend on other parts.

Parts of our environment have developed as a result of millions of years of very slow changes. This is the **natural environment**. The natural environment includes the shape of the land, the climate, and the plants that grow on the land. In Chapters 2, 3, and 4 we will learn about the things that make up the natural environment.

The natural environment.

The human environment.

All over the world there is evidence of people's activities. They have built villages, towns, and cities. They have built cars, aeroplanes, and ships, and the roads, airports, and ports to go with them. People have also changed the plant life (**vegetation**) by farming, mining, logging, and ranching.

The **human environment** includes everything that people have made and also those parts of the natural environment that people have changed. We will learn about the human environment in Chapters 5, 6, and 7.

Location—Where is it?

The location of a place or a thing in the environment is important to the geographer. **Location** is the description of **where** a place or thing is. Read this description of Tau's place in the classroom:

> In Tau's classroom there are five rows of desks, with three desks in each row. The teacher's desk is in front of the middle line of desks. Tau sits at the second desk in the middle line, about three metres in front of the teacher.

Notice that the geographer **first** describes the environment and **then** locates the thing or place in the environment.

Now look at the map of Tau's classroom.

It is much easier to describe location using a map.

This is a simple map. It has a **scale** to show how big the classroom really is. Notice that one unit on the map is **equivalent** to one metre in the classroom. The map also has a **key** which uses **symbols** to represent the main features of the classroom. The map shows only a small area.

Tau's classroom.

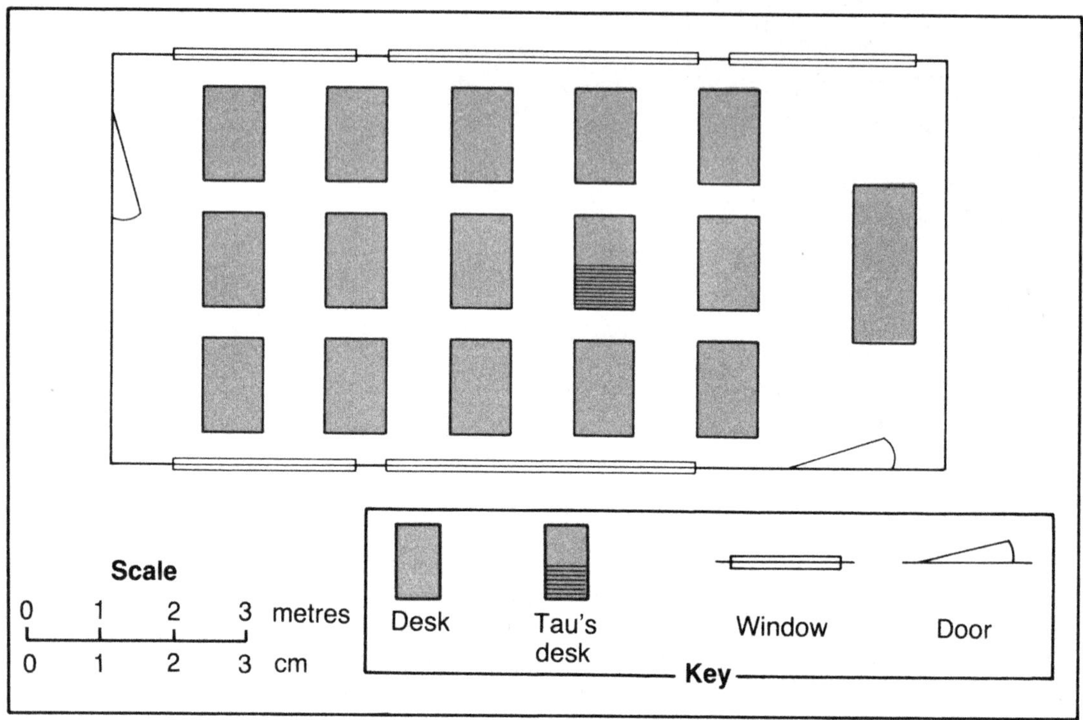

The classroom is part of Kokopo High School in East New Britain Province.

Now study the map on page 3 which shows the location of Kokopo High School in relation to its immediate (nearby) environment.

This map also has a key and a scale. Notice that one centimetre on the map is equivalent to **75 metres** on the ground. This map also shows directions. The direction marker helps to describe the location of the high school in relation to Kokopo Town.

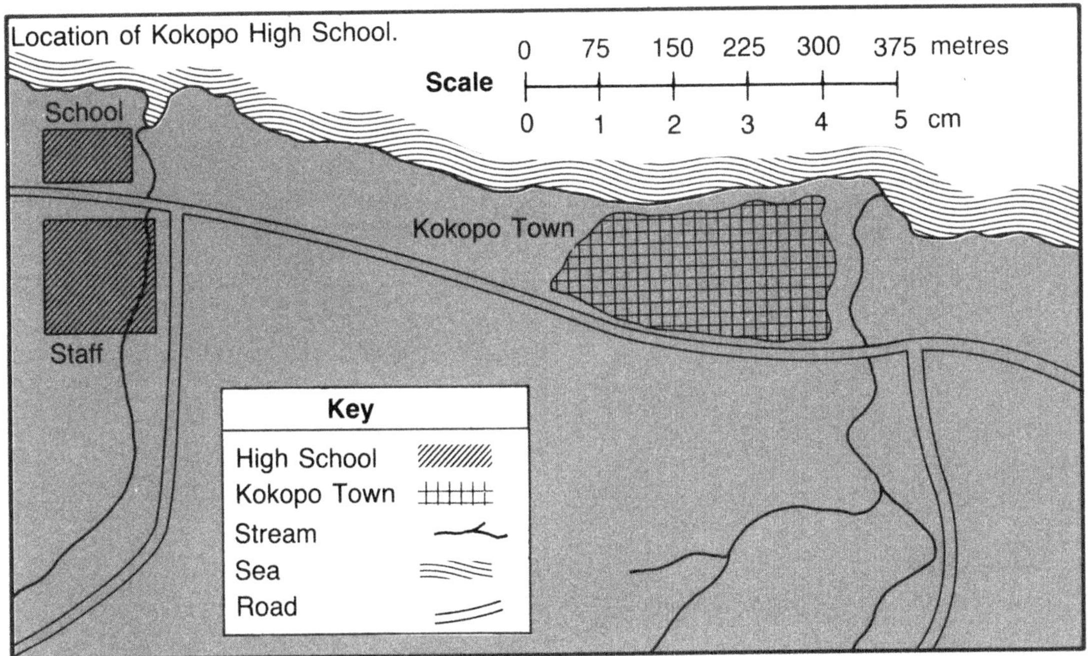

Using all the information on the map we can now describe the location of Kokopo High School.

Kokopo High School is located about **600 metres** to the **west** of Kokopo Town. It is in two parts separated by a road. The part to the **south** is the staff area, and the part to the **north** is the teaching area. This part is less than **100 metres** from the sea.

Where is Kokopo located in East New Britain Province?

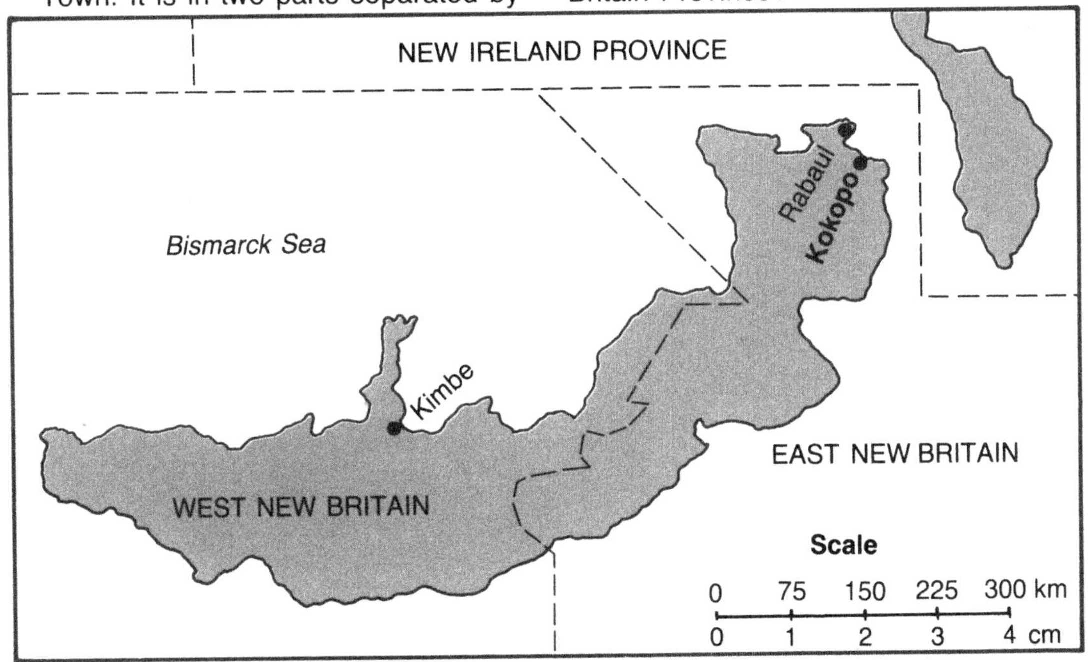

Location of Kokopo in East New Britain Province.

Where is East New Britain located in Papua New Guinea?

Location of East New Britain in Papua New Guinea.

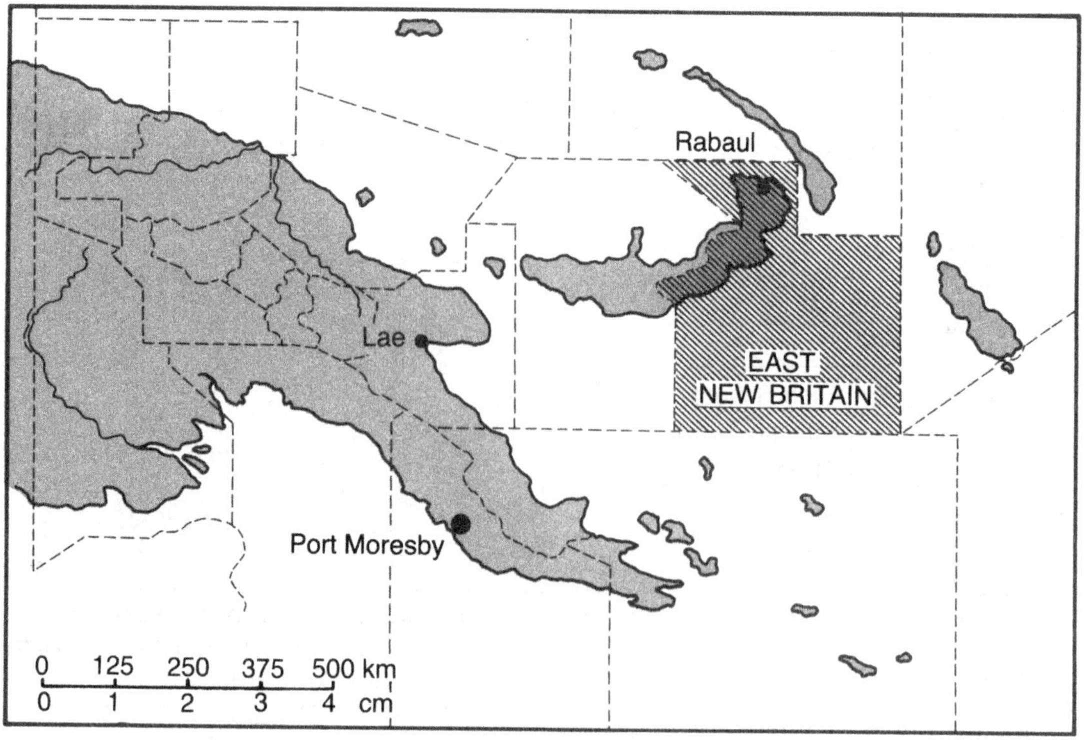

Rabaul
EAST
NEW BRITAIN
Lae
Port Moresby
0 125 250 375 500 km
0 1 2 3 4 cm

Where is Papua New Guinea located in the world?

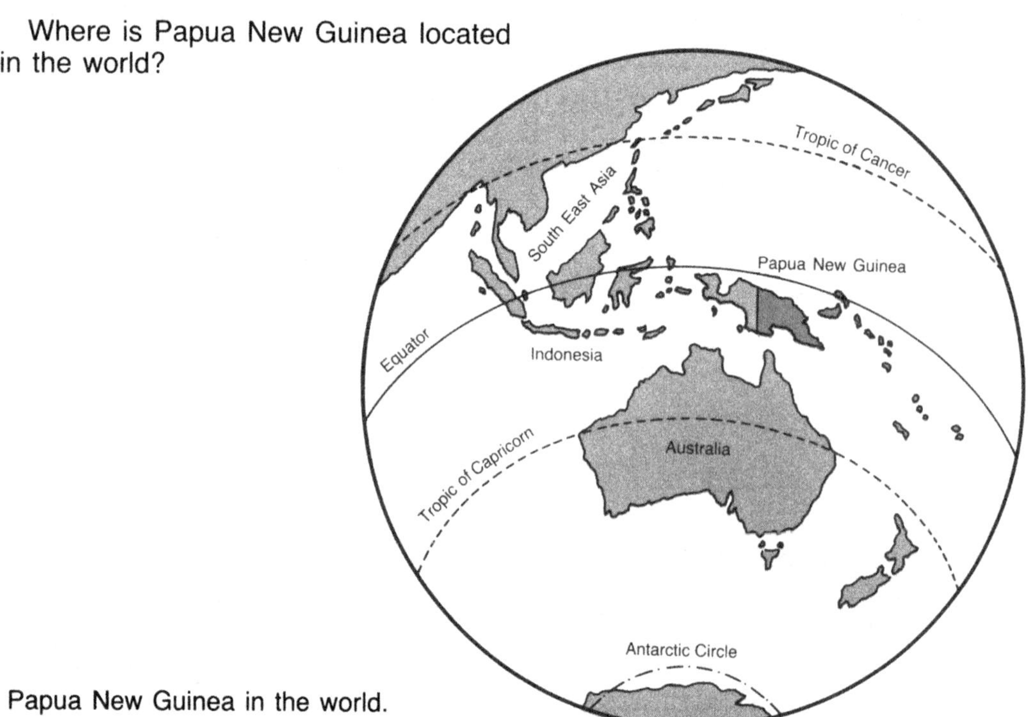

Papua New Guinea in the world.

This picture shows what the world really looks like. The world is a **globe** (or sphere). This picture shows us that Papua New Guinea is located in the same part of the world as Australia and Indonesia. However, this picture shows us only half of the world—the other half is on the other side of the globe.

There are several lines marked on this picture of the world. They run around the globe from **east** to **west**. They are called **lines of latitude**. Only the main lines of latitude have been shown.

The line that runs around the middle of the globe is called the **Equator**. It divides the world into two halves. The southern half is called the **southern hemisphere** (hemi = half; sphere = globe; hemisphere = half a globe). The northern half is called the **northern hemisphere**.

Papua New Guinea is located in the southern hemisphere.

The lines on either side of the Equator

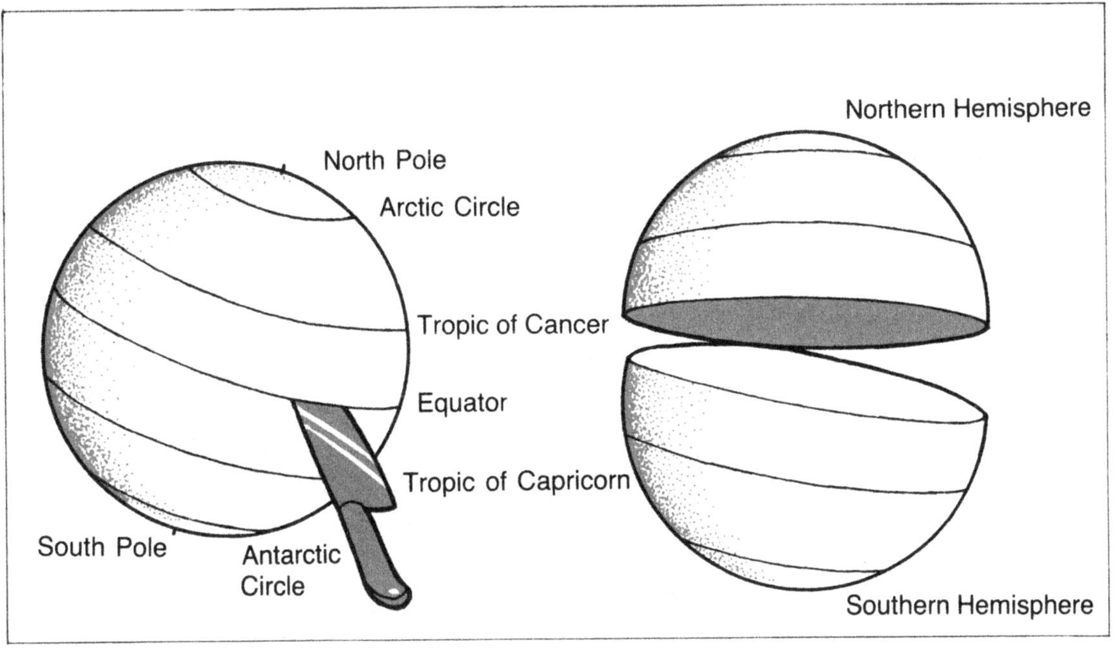

The Equator and the hemispheres.

are called the **tropics**. The line in the southern hemisphere is the **Tropic of Capricorn**, and the line in the northern hemisphere is the **Tropic of Cancer**. Between these two lines the world is generally very hot. Countries located here are known as **tropical countries**.

There are two other lines shown on the diagram above. The one in the southern hemisphere, close to the **South Pole**, is called the **Antarctic Circle**. Places to the south of this line are very cold indeed. The other line is in the northern hemisphere, close to the **North Pole**. It is called the **Arctic Circle**. Places to the north of this line are also very cold indeed. The areas around the south and north poles are covered by ice all the year round. These are **ice caps**.

Places located between the two **polar circles** and the two tropics are called the **temperate** countries. They are neither very hot nor very cold.

A temperate country in Europe.

Drawing Maps

Geographers try to draw the globe on a single sheet of paper to show the location of all the countries in the world. The lines drawn on the globe help them to draw maps which represent the land and the oceans. It is very difficult to draw a round globe on a flat piece of paper. Imagine trying to cut a basketball in half and then laying it flat on the ground! This is what geographers try to do when they draw maps of the world.

The map below shows one way that

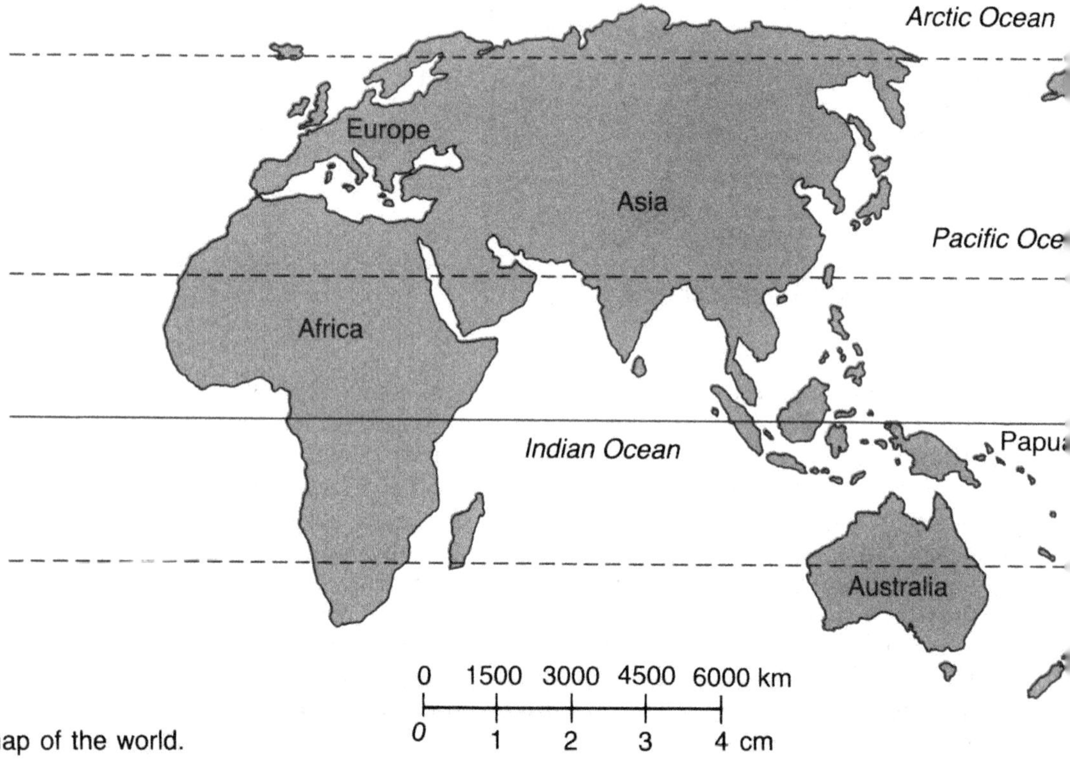

A map of the world.

The Antarctic.

geographers have drawn a map of the world. The major lines of latitude have been drawn to help describe the location of the different places.

The map of the world shows many things. It shows us that the world is made up of land (**continents**) and water (**oceans**). Papua New Guinea is an **island**. It is surrounded by sea. In fact Papua New Guinea is part of the second largest island in the world.

Cold Countries
Much of this area is covered by ice all the year.

Arctic Circle

Temperate Countries
Summers here are hot, often hotter than tropical areas. Winters are cold.

North America

Atlantic Ocean

Tropic of Cancer

Tropical Countries
Climates here are generally hot and wet. Seasonal differences are small.

Guinea

Equator

South America

Tropic of Capricorn

Temperate Countries
There is not much land in this part of the world. Seasonal differences are smaller than in the Northern Hemisphere.

Antarctic Ocean

Papua New Guinea is located in the **southern hemisphere**, between the **Equator** and the **Tropic of Capricorn**. Papua New Guinea is a **tropical** country. To the south of Papua New Guinea is the **continent** of Australia. To the east is the **Pacific Ocean**.

Summary of Main Ideas

When describing the location of a place we can use maps.

Maps tell us many things:
- the size of the place, and how far from one place to another (scale)
- what things are in the place (key)
- the direction of one place from another (direction marker)
- the shape of a place.

In the next three chapters we will look at ways of describing the environment of Papua New Guinea.

Activities

Exercises

1. Fill in the missing words in the paragraph below.

   Everything around us makes up the ________. The ________ environment is everything that has not been changed by people. Whenever people change the area around them it becomes part of the ________ environment. The study of the environment is called ________. We can use ________ as well as words and pictures to describe the environment.

2. Draw a simple map of your classroom similar to the one shown on page 2. Remember to include a scale and a key. Show the location of your desk by using a cross.

   How far is it from your desk to the teacher's desk:

   (a) on the ground in your classroom? (in metres)

   (b) on your map? (in centimetres)

3. In a short paragraph, describe the location of your school. Include the following in your description:

   (a) the part of the province the school is in,

   (b) the distance to the nearest town,

   (c) the direction of the school **from** the nearest town,

   (d) the location of the school with respect to any other obvious features, e.g. the coast, a high mountain.

4. Study the maps of the classroom (page 2), Kokopo (page 3), East New Britain (page 3) and Papua New Guinea (page 4).

   Now complete the following table:

Distance on the Map	**Distance on the Ground**			
	Classroom	**Kokopo**	**East New Britain**	**Papua New Guinea**
1 cm	1 metre			
2 cm		150 metres		
2·5 cm			187·5 km	

5. Fill in the blanks in the following paragraph:

   The world is shaped like a ______. The lines that are drawn around the globe from east to ________ are called lines of ________. Hot countries are found between the ________ ________ ________ and the ________ ________ ________. Near the south and north poles the countries have ________ climates.

6. Study your atlas and the world map on pages 6–7 very carefully and then answer the questions that follow.

   (a) List four countries that the equator passes through.

   (b) What is the name of the tropic that passes through Australia?

   (c) How far is it from Port Moresby to Singapore?

   (d) What direction is Hawaii from Papua New Guinea?

   (e) In which hemisphere is Europe located?

   (f) What ocean separates Asia from North America?

   (g) Name two countries from the warm (temperate) region of the world.

(h) Which continents have land in **both** the northern and the southern hemispheres?

(i) For each of the following countries, use your school atlas to find where they are located, and write down whether they are **hot**, **cold**, or **temperate** countries.

- **(i)** Greenland
- **(ii)** Argentina
- **(iii)** Tanzania
- **(iv)** France
- **(v)** Sri Lanka
- **(vi)** New Zealand
- **(vii)** Israel
- **(viii)** Japan

Things to Do

1. The top photograph on page 1 shows an example of the natural environment. Write a list of five things that you can see in the photograph that are part of the natural environment.

2. The bottom photograph on page 1 shows an example of the human environment. Write a list of five things that you can see in the photograph that are part of the human environment.

3. On a blank map of Papua New Guinea (showing province boundaries) colour in your home province. Put a dot, and label it, to show where your school is located.

(a) How far is it from your school to Port Moresby?

(b) What direction is Port Moresby from your school?

4. Collect pictures and newspaper clippings about the environment. Make a display on the wall of your classroom to show the differences between the human and natural environments.

2. The Natural Environment: Landforms

The Shape of the Land

Papua New Guinea is a **mountainous** country. The mountains mainly form a **chain** along the centre of the island. The coastal regions are usually much flatter and are called **lowlands**. Many large rivers flow from the mountains and across the lowlands to the sea. There are also many smaller islands that form a part of Papua New Guinea. Geographers use the word **landforms** to mean the shape of the land.

This map shows the **highland** and **lowland** areas of Papua New Guinea and also some of the large rivers that flow to the sea.

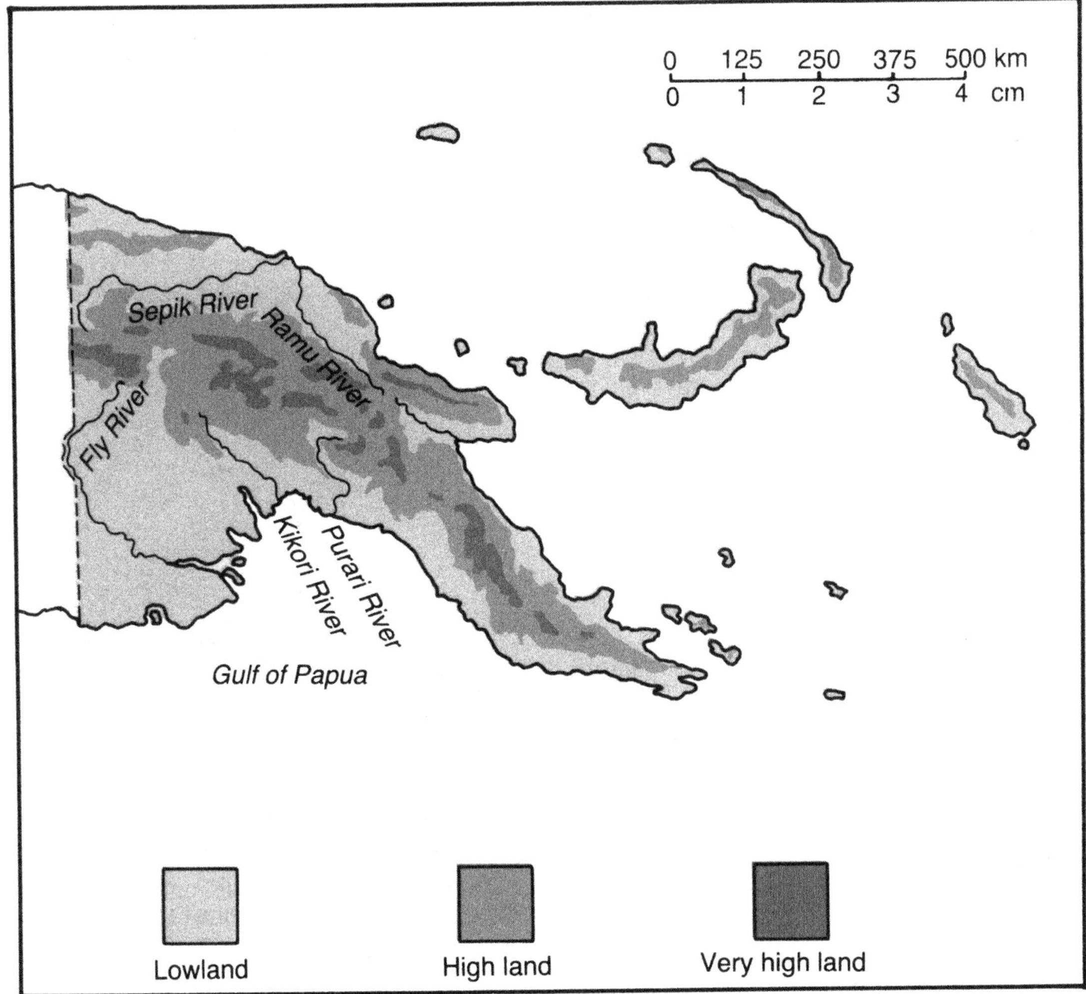

Landforms of Papua New Guinea.

Photographs can be used to help describe the landforms of Papua New Guinea. Look at the following examples and work out which part of the map they could be from.

Highland Valley

The mountainous areas of Papua New Guinea have large valleys running through them. Many people live in these valleys.

Island

This is one of the many islands off the coast of Papua New Guinea. Some of these islands are flat, but many of them are mountainous like this one.

Mountains

Notice how rugged (steep-sided) these mountains are. What signs of human occupation can you see?

Coastal Lowland

The land here is flat with some gently rolling hills. Many people live here, and many crops are grown.

The map on page 11 shows you where most of the mountains in Papua New Guinea are located. The photographs above show you what mountainous regions look like. Because the mountains are so steep and rugged they are difficult places for people to live. Most people build their houses in the valleys.

How Mountains and Valleys are Formed

Before we can explain how the mountains and valleys were formed, we must first look at the structure of the world. The diagram below shows what the earth (world) would look like if it was cut in half.

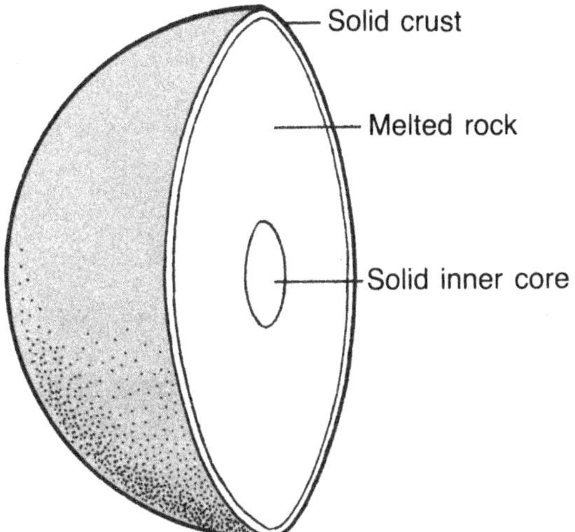

The structure of the Earth.

The inside of the earth is very hot and is like a thick, sticky liquid. This is because it is so hot that the rocks there have melted. The part of the earth that makes up the land surface is a very thin layer of **solid** rock. This is called the **crust**. The crust is so thin that it bends and cracks when the melted rock inside the earth moves. This causes changes in the shape of the land.

Mountains and valleys can be caused by the **folding** of the layers of rock in the crust. This happens when movements of the melted rock inside the earth make the crust bend.

Folded rocks near Tatana, N.C.D.

How mountains and valleys are formed by folding.

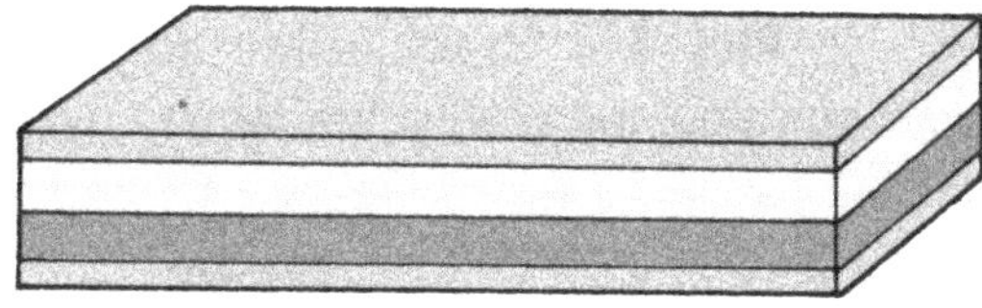

Before folding the land is flat.

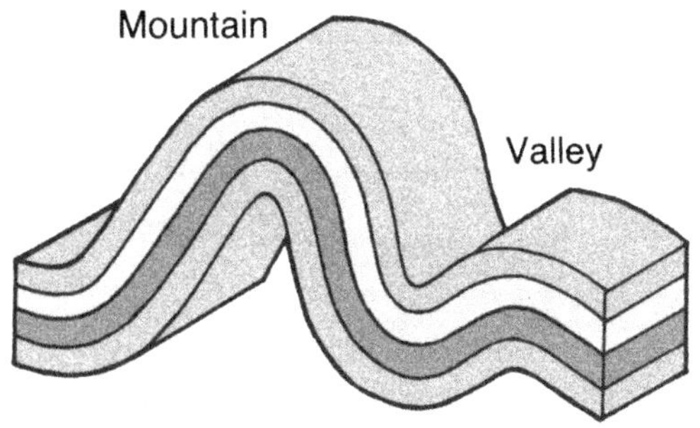

After folding the land is pushed up to form mountains and valleys.

Folded rocks.

The Wahgi Valley. This valley was formed by folding.

Mountains and valleys can also be formed by the **faulting** of layers of the crust. A **fault** is a crack in the crust of the earth caused by melted rock moving inside the earth.

How mountains and valleys are formed by faulting.

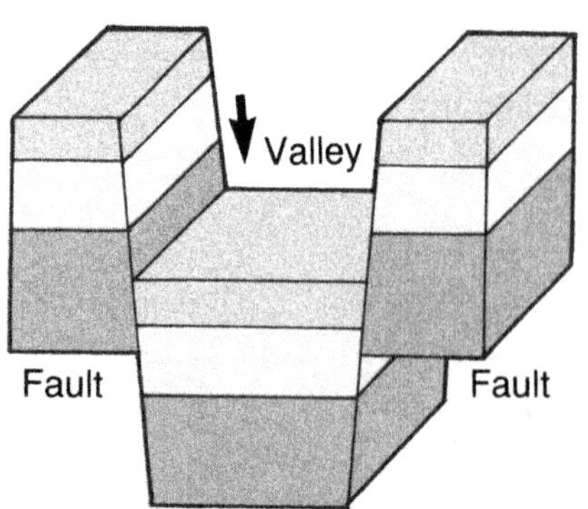

Here the land has slipped down between two cracks (faults).

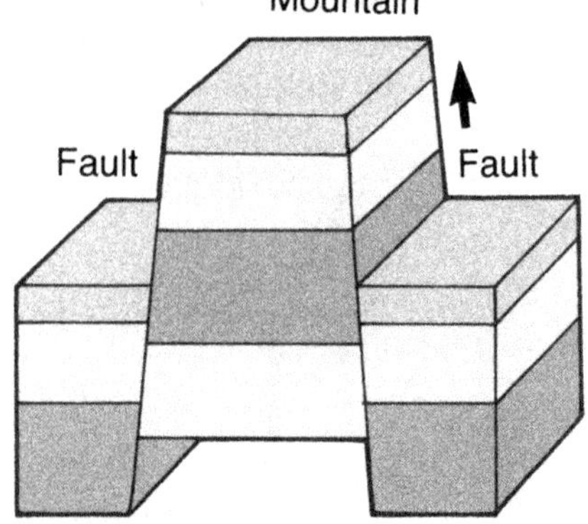

Here the land is pushed up between two cracks (faults).

Faulted rocks.

The Markham Valley. This valley was formed by faulting.

Mountains can also be formed by **volcanoes**. Volcanoes are found where the melted rock inside the earth comes to the surface through cracks in the crust.

When the melted rock comes to the surface we say that the volcano is **erupting**. Very often large rocks and clouds of dust and ashes are thrown out of the volcano at the same time. **Earthquakes** usually occur when a volcano erupts.

Volcanoes in Rabaul erupting in 1937.

How mountains are formed by volcanoes.

Crack in the crust

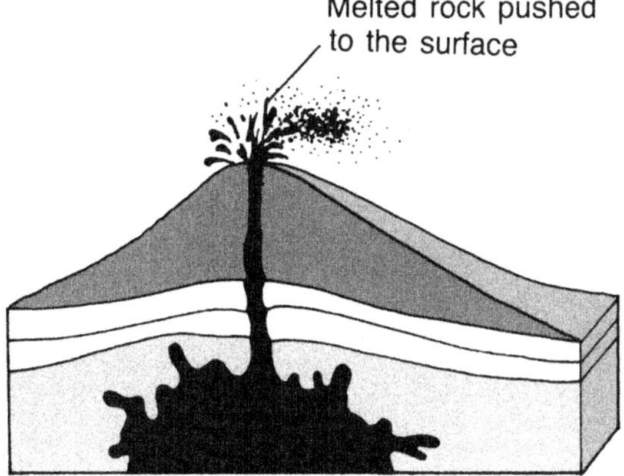

Before erupting.

Melted rock is pushed to the surface

After erupting.

Mountain is formed as melted rock cools to form solid rock on the surface.

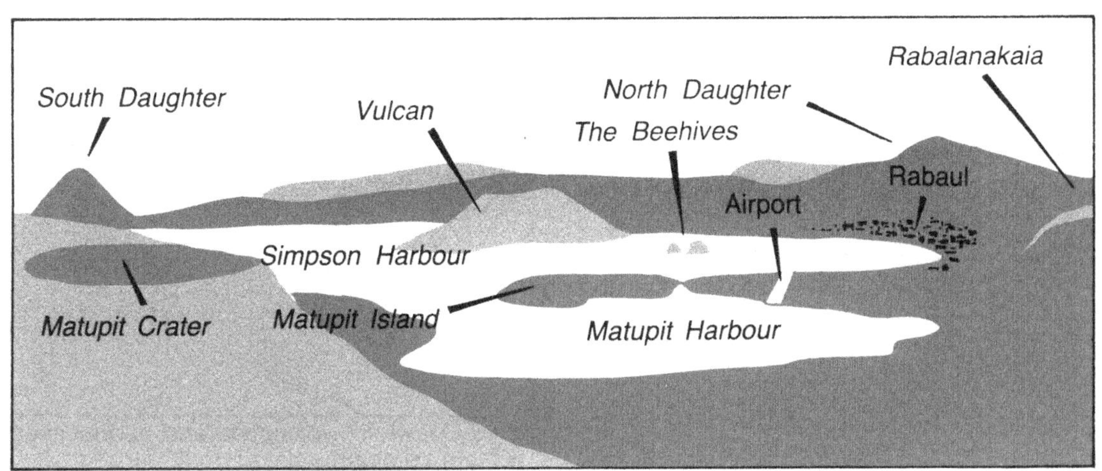

Rabaul and its volcanoes in 1986: the view from the top of Matupit volcano.

There are many volcanoes in Papua New Guinea today. The map below shows where some of them are located.

The main volcanoes in Papua New Guinea.

0 125 250 375 500 km
0 1 2 3 4 cm

Active volcano (date of last definite eruption)
Volcano observatory
Extinct volcano

Pacific Ocean
Solomon Sea
Tuluman (1953–7)
Blupblup
Bam (1954–60)
Manam (1977)
Submarine (1951?)
Karkar (1978)
Long I. (1975)
Langila (1977)
Talo
Ritter I. (1974)
Narage
Garove
Bola
Submarine (1970?)
Rabaul (1943)
Lolo
Pago
Ulawun (1985)
Bamus (19th C.?)
Balbi (19th C.?)
Bagana (1976–7)
Doma Peaks
Yelia
Lamington (1951–2)
Kururi
Victory
Goropu (1943–4)
Lamonai, Oiau, Dobu

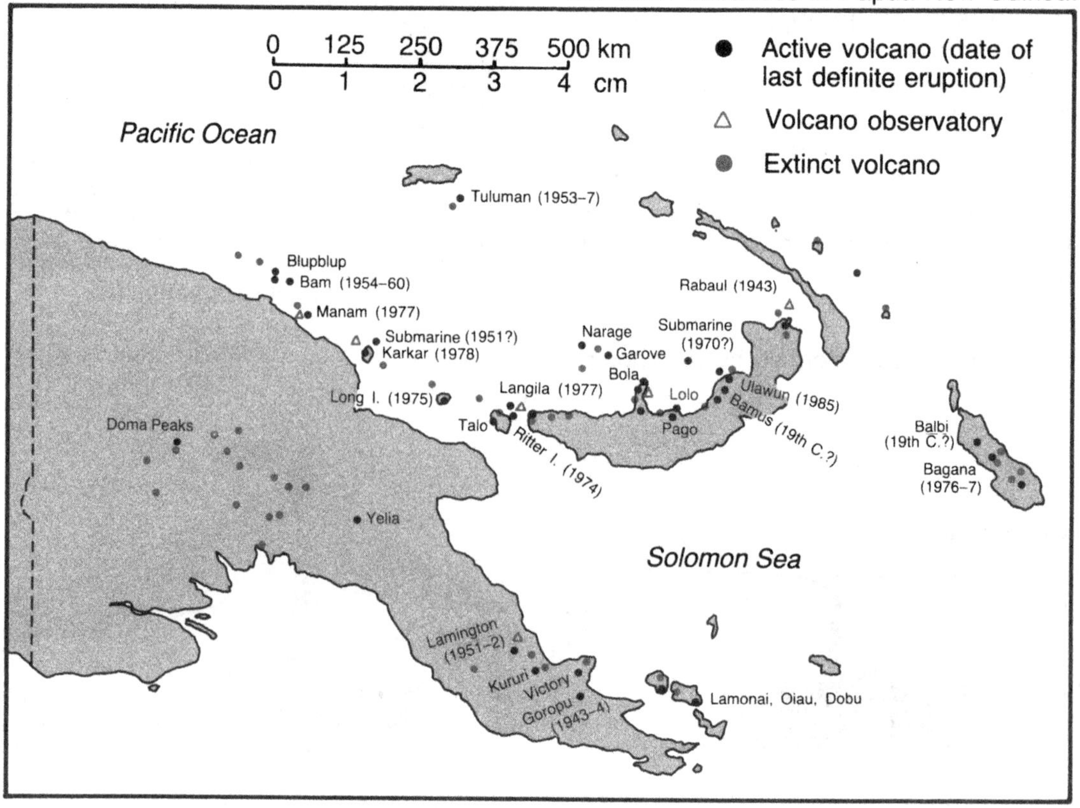

Many of Papua New Guinea's mountainous islands have been formed by volcanoes. The photograph on page 12 is one of these islands. Other islands, which are flatter, have been formed by coral. Often the coral grows on volcanoes under the sea.

Papua New Guinea is part of a large chain of volcanoes that runs right around the edge of the Pacific Ocean. This is known as the Pacific "Ring of Fire".

Area where volcanoes and earthquakes are common.

The Pacific "Ring of Fire".

An earthquake in Mexico City in 1985.

The Work of Rivers

If you look at the map on page 11 you can see the location of the major rivers of Papua New Guinea. All these rivers flow from highland areas to lowland areas. Rivers flow in **valleys**. Some of these valleys have been formed by folding or faulting; other valleys have been made by the rivers themselves.

Valleys in the Highlands are very steep and the rivers flow very fast. The river carries gravel and small pebbles with it. These stones slowly wear away the bottom of the river. This is called **erosion**. The rock that is worn away is carried by the rivers to the lowlands.

Highland river valley.

Lowland river valley.

Lowland river valleys are not very steep and the water flows very slowly. Because the water moves so slowly it cannot carry as much of the rock that was worn away in the Highlands. Much of this rock, by now broken up into small pieces, is dropped by the river. This is called **deposition**. The mud and soil that is deposited is called **alluvium**.

Lowlands

Many lowland areas are formed by the **deposition** of worn-down rock, mud, and soil. **Swamps** are formed where water cannot drain away quickly. People have difficulty living in swampy areas.

But lowland areas near rivers are useful to people. The land is flat and so it is easy to build houses. Also the deposited soil from the rivers (**alluvium**) is very fertile and good for growing crops.

Lowland rivers such as the Sepik and the Fly are useful to people because canoes and boats can travel a long way on them. This is because the rivers are very wide and slow moving.

Swamp.

Summary of Main Ideas

Papua New Guinea has a variety of landforms:

- mountains are formed by folding, faulting, and volcanoes
- valleys are formed by folding, faulting, and the work of rivers
- rivers wear away (erode) rock in the highland areas
- lowlands are formed from eroded rock (alluvium) deposited by rivers.

The landforms of Papua New Guinea can be described using maps, photographs, and sketches. Diagrams are useful to explain how things happen.

Activities

Exercises

1. Fill in the blanks in the following paragraph:

   Irian Jaya and Papua New Guinea are parts of the ________ largest island in the world. Papua New Guinea has many ________ which form a chain along the ________ of the main island. These mountains are mainly formed by the bending and cracking of the earth's ________. These processes are called ________ and ________. Many of Papua New Guinea's smaller islands are formed by ________.

2. Answer the following questions:
   (a) What is the solid, surface layer of the earth called?
   (b) How was the Markham Valley formed?
   (c) What type of mountain is Mount Lamington?
   (d) What is the name given to the washing away of soil by rivers?
   (e) List three reasons why rivers are useful to people.

3. Imagine you were in Rabaul in 1937. Write a short story describing what you would have seen when Vulcan and Matupit erupted. (Clue: look at the drawing and photograph on page 15.)

Things to Discuss

1. Why are swampy areas not good places to live?

Things to Do

1. Locate your school on the landforms map on page 11. What landform region is your school located in?
2. Draw a sketch of the landforms of the area around your school.
3. Make models out of clay, Plasticine, or paper, to show how folding or faulting may occur. Write your explanation in your notebook.
4. Collect newspaper clippings about events that have happened in some of the areas mentioned in this chapter. Stick the clippings in your notebook and explain how the event affected the people in the area (e.g. a volcanic eruption).
5. Find out what the emergency procedures are in the case of an earthquake or volcanic eruption. Practise a drill!
6. Look at the volcanoes map on page 16. Name the three volcanoes that are closest to your school. How many kilometres away are they?
7. Visit a river. Find out which parts of the river are eroding material and which parts are depositing material.
8. Copy the puzzle below into your books and find the following words:

   alluvium erosion fault river
   swamp valley volcano

   When you find them, colour them in to make them stand out clearly. Two words are back to front.

B	Z	K	G	O	E	Y	E	Q
G	A	H	R	E	V	I	R	L
A	L	L	V	N	O	S	O	Y
R	L	W	A	Q	G	J	S	K
S	U	P	L	Y	F	A	I	R
R	V	O	L	C	A	N	O	A
X	I	P	E	T	U	O	N	A
O	U	E	Y	U	L	I	N	E
P	M	A	W	S	T	R	O	T

3. The Natural Environment: Weather and Climate

Weather

"It was very hot today. There was very little wind and the humidity was high. Clouds started to appear in the middle of the afternoon and there was a heavy rainstorm that lasted for one hour in the evening."

The passage above describes the **weather** of a typical day in Papua New Guinea. Words like cloudy, misty, windy, wet, dry, stormy, cold, hot, sunny, humid, and dull can all be used to describe the weather.

Weather is the picture of rain, sun, wind, cloud, humidity, and heat that can be described **every day**. One day can be very different from the next.

Geographers observe the weather by measuring rainfall using a rain gauge and by recording temperatures using a thermometer. They also find out which way the wind is blowing and look at how much cloud there is in the sky.

Weather Recordings for One Week from Kokopo High School

	Monday	Tuesday	Wednesday	Thursday	Friday	Saturday	Sunday
Rainfall (mm)	10	5	–	–	22	33	8
Highest (maximum) temperature (°C)	31	31	32	32	30	29	31
Lowest (minimum) temperature (°C)	24	24	22	23	24	25	24
Wind direction (from)	NW	NW	no wind	no wind	NW	NW	N

The records in the table can be shown more clearly as graphs. Temperature readings are best shown as **line graphs**.

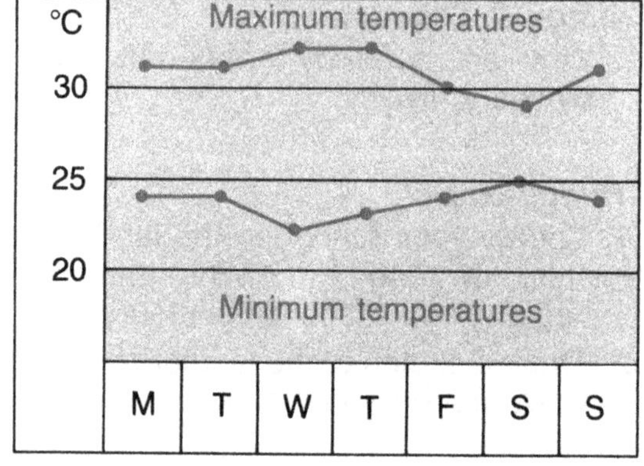

Maximum and minimum temperatures for one week.

Rainfall measurements can best be shown as **column graphs**.

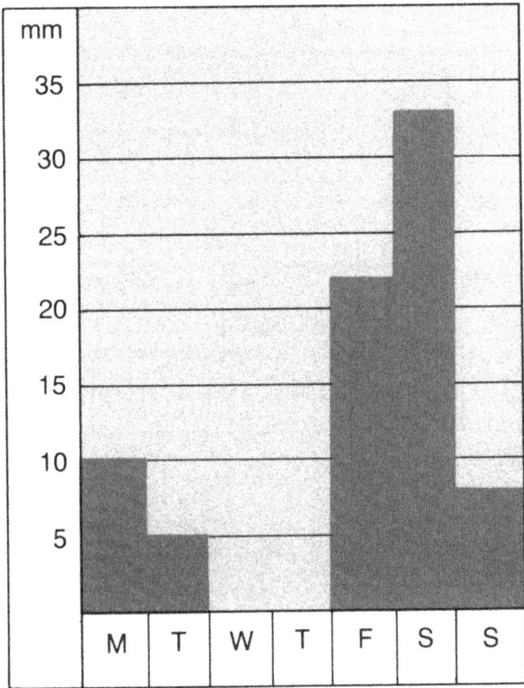

Rainfall for one week.

Weather can affect the things people do **every day**.

"I usually go to the garden every day, but it rained so hard yesterday that I stayed in the house."

"I planned to go fishing last night, but the wind was too strong so I went hunting instead."

Climate

Geographers use daily measurements to find **patterns** in the weather. Measurements made over many years show that regular changes occur in the pattern of weather throughout the year. These patterns can be different from place to place. The name given to these weather **patterns** is **climate**.

Climate Figures for Madang												
	J	**F**	**M**	**A**	**M**	**J**	**J**	**A**	**S**	**O**	**N**	**D**
Rainfall (mm)	359	292	344	443	337	209	166	128	144	301	387	379
Temperature (°C)	27	27	27	27	27	26	26	26	26	26	27	27

Climate Figures for Goroka												
	J	**F**	**M**	**A**	**M**	**J**	**J**	**A**	**S**	**O**	**N**	**D**
Rainfall (mm)	230	254	265	204	113	54	49	74	121	154	171	243
Temperature (°C)	21	21	21	21	21	20	19	20	20	20	20	21

These figures are the **average** of measurements taken over a period of many years.

The figures shown in the tables can best be shown as **climate graphs**.

Average monthly temperatures.

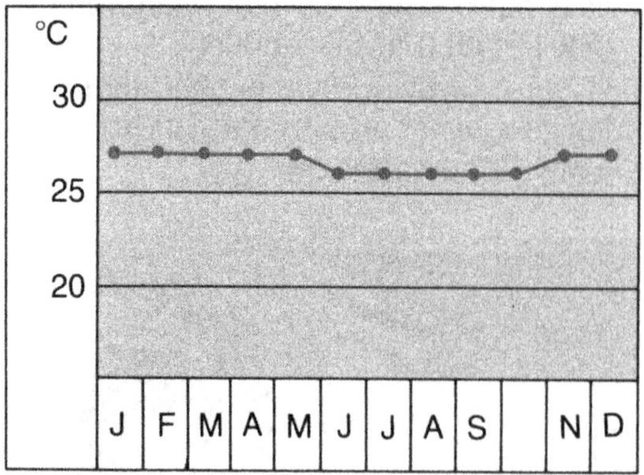

Madang

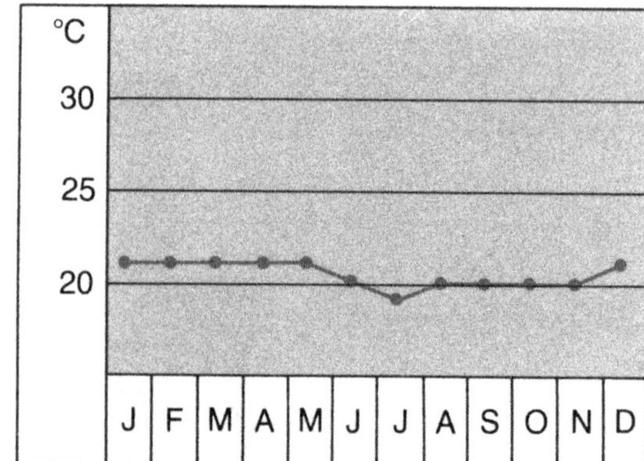

Goroka

Average monthly rainfall.

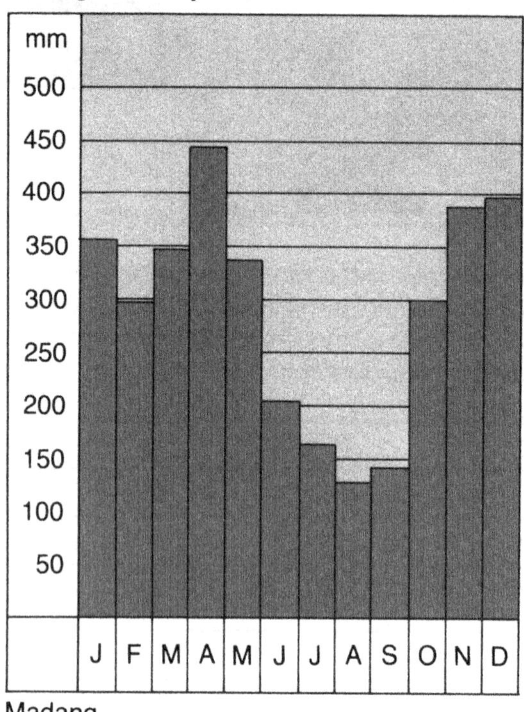

Madang

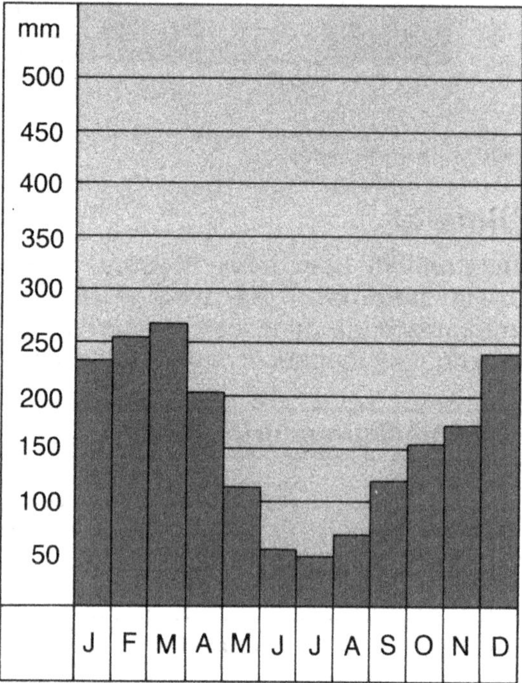

Goroka

When we compare the graphs for Madang and Goroka, we can see that both towns have some things in common, but that other things are different.

Both towns have a cooler, less wet (drier) **season** from June to October. However, on average, Madang is both hotter and wetter than Goroka.

What Makes Climates Different?

Papua New Guinea has a **tropical climate**. It is generally hot and wet all the year round. However, if we look at climate figures for different places, we can see that the climate varies slightly from place to place.

Look at the following map which shows the different climates of Papua New Guinea.

Differences in winds and landforms cause climates to vary from one place to another.

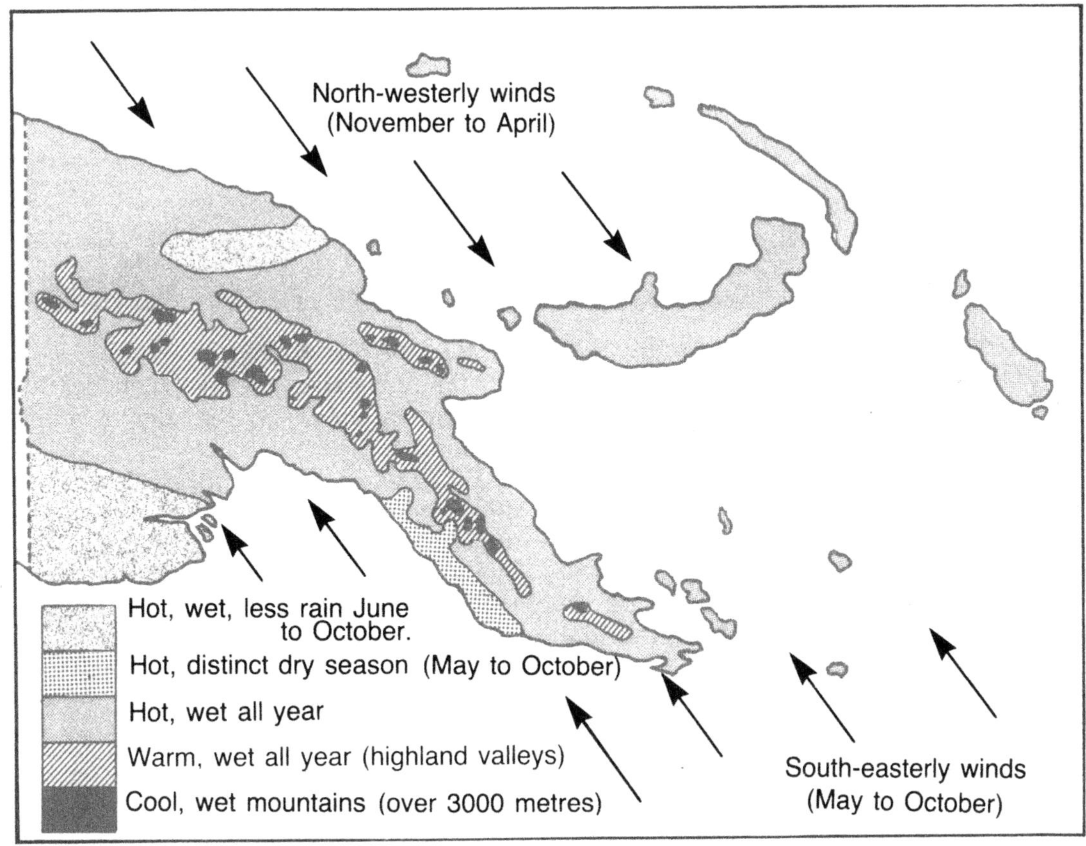

Climate regions of Papua New Guinea.

Wind

Papua New Guinea has two main winds that blow at different times of the year.

From **November to April** the winds blow mainly **from the north-west**. They bring a lot of rain with them.

From **May to October** the winds blow mainly **from the south-east**. They bring rain to some parts of the country but not to others. This is the time when Port Moresby has a very dry season.

Landforms

Look at the map of Papua New Guinea's landforms on page 11 and compare it with the map above. We can see that the highland areas have rain all the year round. Generally, more rain falls in the highland areas than in the lowland areas.

We can also see that the highland areas are not as hot as the lowland areas.

This is because **temperature decreases as height (altitude) increases.**

How temperature decreases as height increases.

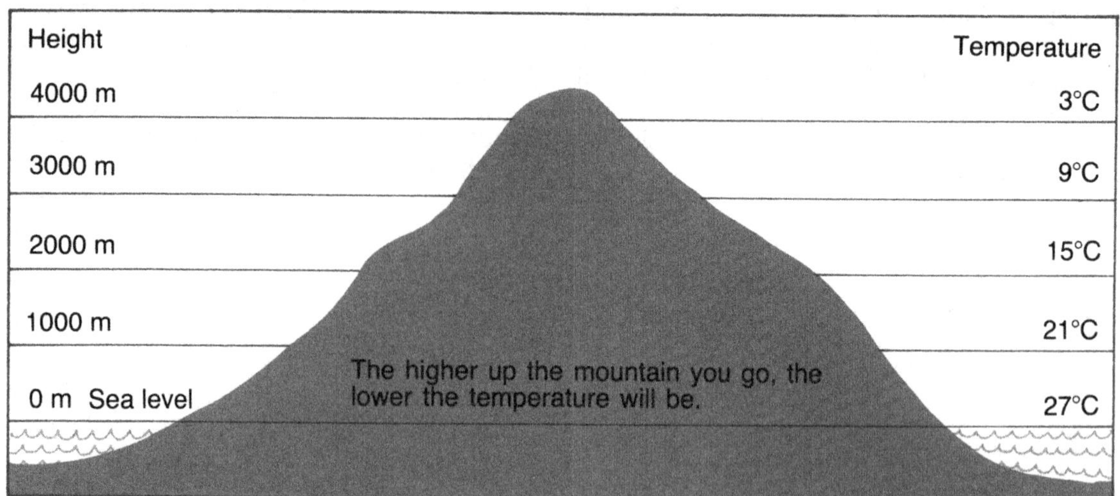

All of these changes in climate are very important to people. Knowing about changes in weather and climate can help people plan their activities. For example, people on the coast would want to know what clothes to wear for a visit to the Highlands, or when strong winds would make fishing difficult. The climate can also affect the type of houses that people build as well as the way they live.

A Horizon Calendar

In many regions people can tell the season by watching the sun at sunset or sunrise.

By watching the sun at sunset the Motu people knew when to set sail on their great Hiri trading expeditions. In the same way, farmers know when to expect the wet season and when to plant or harvest their crops.

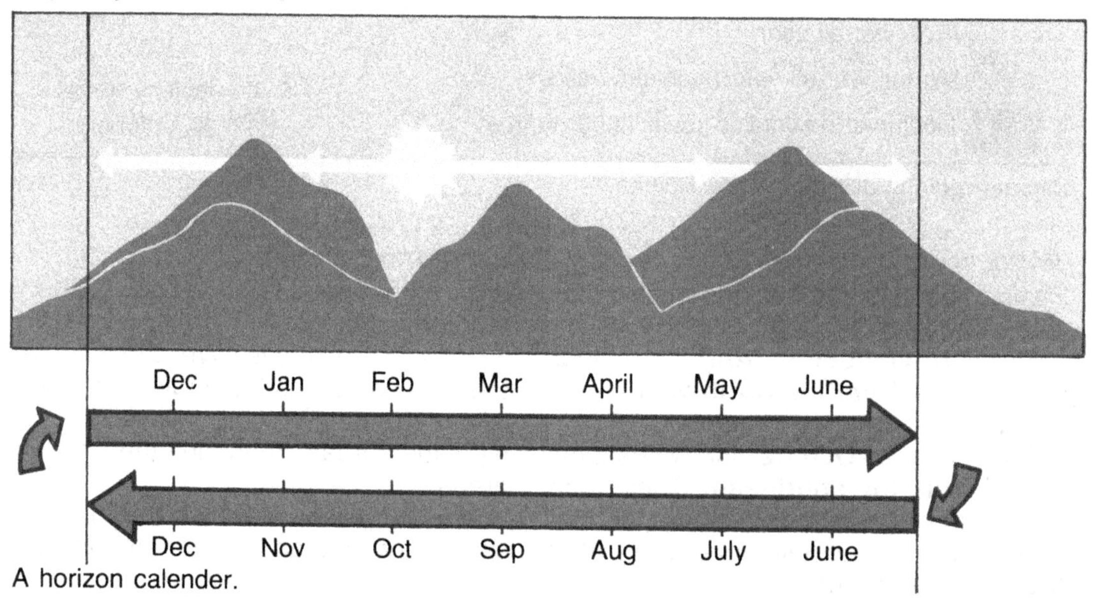

A horizon calender.

Natural Hazards

Sometimes the weather can be different from what people expect.

Flood

In some seasons there is a lot more rainfall than is usual. This causes **floods**. This photograph shows a flood in a lowland river valley. The houses are surrounded by flood waters.

Floods can cause landslides and wash away houses and food gardens. The photograph below shows the erosion caused by a river in Lae when it flooded.

Erosion caused by a flood.

Frost

Sometimes it can be colder than usual. If this happens in the Highlands the ground may become frozen during the coldest part of the night. This is called **frost** and it can badly damage the food gardens and the valuable coffee crops grown there.

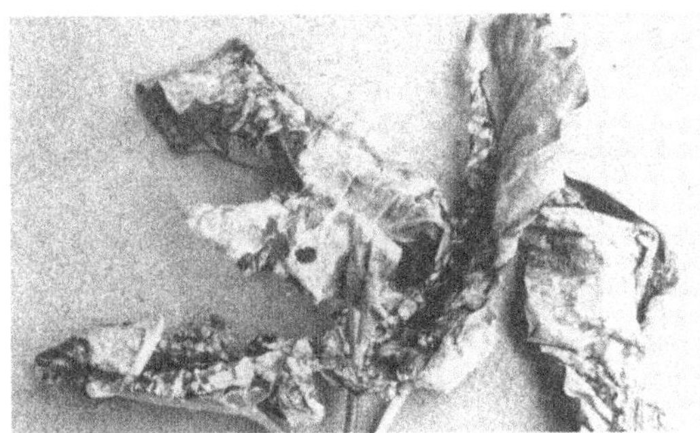

A plant damaged by frost.

A flood in a lowland river valley.

Drought

In some seasons there is less rain than usual. This causes a **drought**. This means that there is not enough water to grow crops. The ground becomes hard and difficult to dig.

There was a long drought in Port Moresby between 1981 and 1983. The low level of water in nearby reservoirs meant that people in Port Moresby had to use less water. They could not water their gardens.

Dry, cracked soil in a drought.

Summary of Main Ideas

Weather is the **day to day** amounts of rainfall, cloud, sunshine, wind, and temperature.

Climate is the **pattern** of rainfall and temperature over a long period of time.

Climate in Papua New Guinea **varies** from place to place because of:

- changing wind patterns,
- the different landforms,
- how high the land is.

Both weather and climate affect the way people live.

Natural hazards of climate are:

- floods,
- droughts,
- frost.

Natural hazards can seriously affect the way people live.

Activities

Exercises

1. Choose the correct statement to complete the sentence:

   Climate is the word that is used to describe

   A. how much rain a place gets.
   B. the overall pattern of rain and temperature.
   C. how much sun a place gets.
   D. mist-covered mountains.

2. Choose the correct statement to complete the sentence:

   A climate graph shows

   A. weather patterns for each day in a month.
   B. the overall pattern of sunshine.
   C. how much rain falls and the average temperature for each month.
   D. the overall pattern of cloud.

3. Which word is not directly associated with climate?

   A. sunshine
   B. temperature
   C. rain
   D. people

4. Rearrange the letters to make proper words, then use each of them in a separate sentence.

   (a) acmteli
   (b) inra
   (c) htea
   (d) trateurepme
   (e) thwerea

5. Study the climate graphs on page 22, and then fill in the blanks in the following sentences:

   (a) Temperature is measured in ________.
   (b) Rainfall is measured in ________.
   (c) The letters at the bottom stand for the ________ of the ________.
   (d) Each line on the rainfall graph is worth ________ mm.
   (e) Each line on the temperature graph is worth ________°C.
   (f) In Goroka, about ________ mm of rain falls in July.
   (g) The average temperature in Madang in December is ____°C.

Things to Discuss

1. Use the following headings to describe the climate of your area:

   (a) sunshine during the year
   (b) temperature in the different seasons (does it change much?)
   (c) rainfall (when is the wet season and when is the dry season?).

2. How does the climate affect the people in your area? Visit a village or talk to some local village elders and find out how rainfall and temperature patterns affect them. For example, planting and harvesting crops, building a new house, going swimming.

3. What is the difference between climate and weather?

Things to Do

1. Keep a record of the weather at your school for one week by filling in the table below. What other information could you record? (Hint: how much cloud was there?)

	Monday	Tuesday	Wednesday	Thursday	Friday	Saturday	Sunday
Rainfall (mm)							
Highest (maximum) temperature (°C)							
Lowest (minimum) temperature (°C)							
Wind direction (from)							

2. Look at the climate graphs for Madang on page 22. Use the following words to describe the climate of Madang.
   (a) Temperature: hot, cold, very hot, warm.
   (b) Rainfall: very wet, wet, dry.
   (c) When is the wet season?
   (d) When is the dry season?
   Now do the same for Goroka.

3. Copy the following figures of temperature and rainfall for Port Moresby into your book.

Climate Figures for Port Moresby												
	J	**F**	**M**	**A**	**M**	**J**	**J**	**A**	**S**	**O**	**N**	**D**
Rainfall (mm)	119	239	217	143	41	41	16	31	37	37	48	145
Temperature (° C)	28	27	27	27	27	26	26	26	26	27	28	28

Copy the following grids and use them to draw climate graphs for Port Moresby:

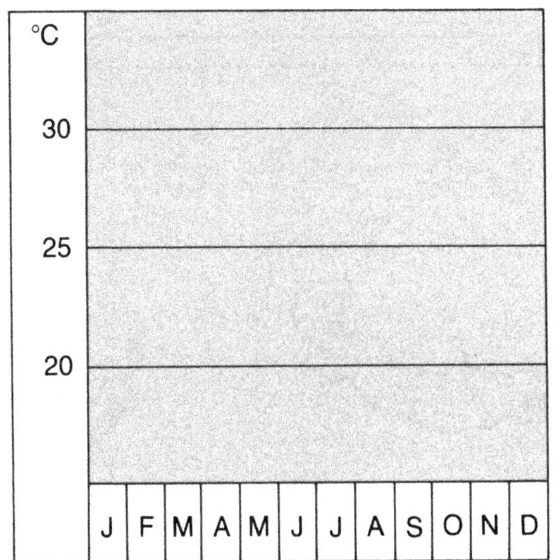

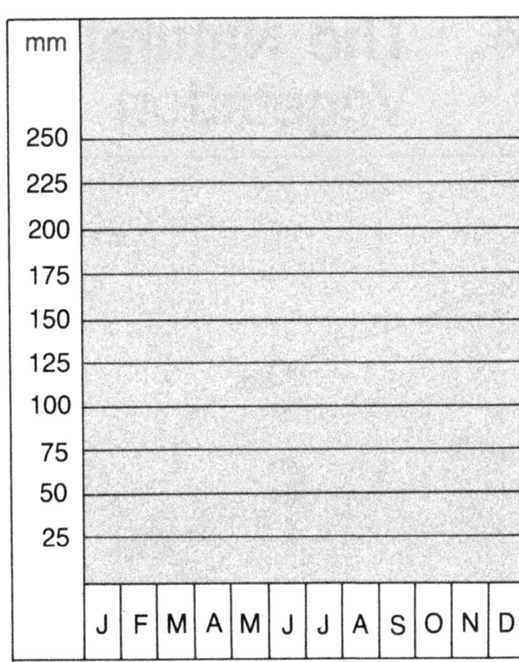

4. Answer the following questions based on the figures above and the graphs you have just drawn.

(a) In one or two sentences, describe the climate of Port Moresby.

(b) Which is the hottest month in Port Moresby?
What is that temperature?

(c) Which is the coldest month in Port Moresby?
What is that temperature?

(d) Which is the wettest month in Port Moresby?
How much rain is there?

(e) Which is the driest month in Port Moresby?
How much rain is there?

(f) How is the climate of Port Moresby different from that of Madang?

5. Geographers like to know how **different** the highest and the lowest temperatures are. The difference between the highest temperature and the lowest temperature is called the **temperature range**. We will work out the range for Madang together.

Madang

The highest temperature = 28°C
The lowest temperature = 26°C
Difference between highest and lowest = 28°C − 26°C = 2°C
Range = 2°C

Now do the same for Port Moresby and Goroka.

4. The Natural Environment: Vegetation

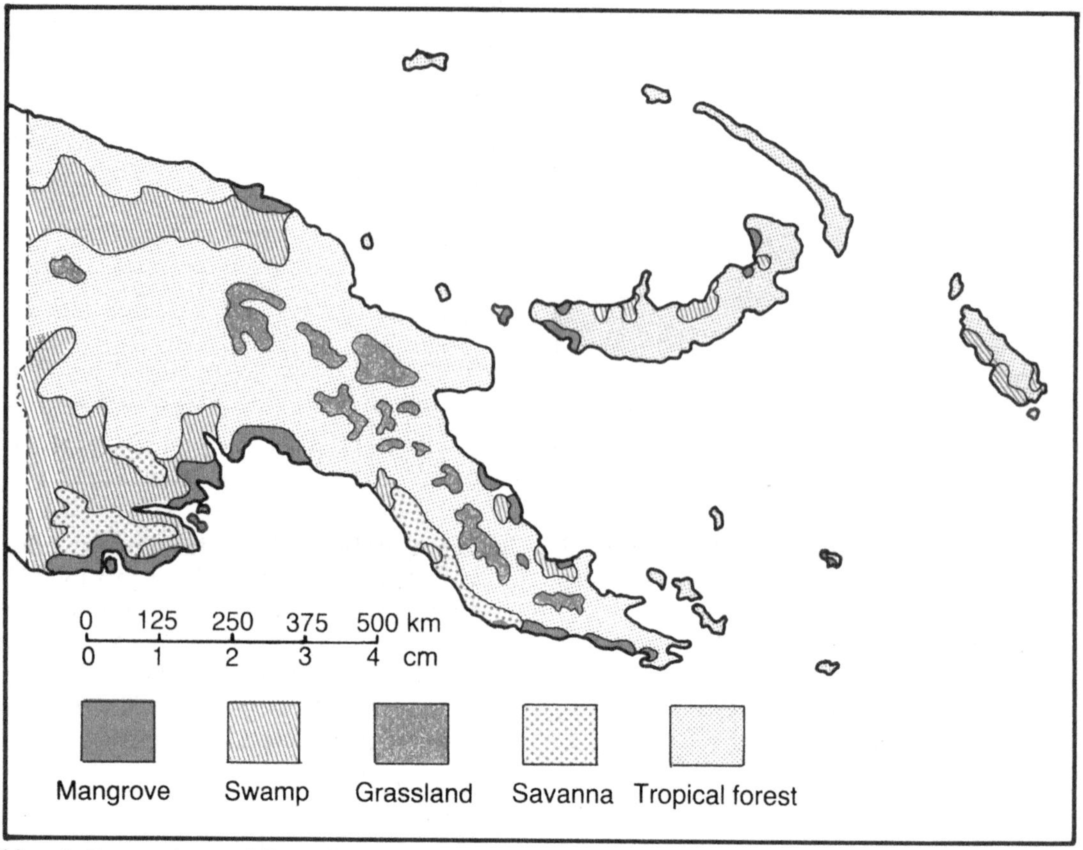

0 125 250 375 500 km
0 1 2 3 4 cm
Mangrove
Swamp
Grassland
Savanna
Tropical forest

Vegetation regions of Papua New Guinea.

The **vegetation** of an area is made up of the **plants** that grow there.

In Papua New Guinea there are several different types of vegetation. This is because there are different landform regions and climate regions.

The type of vegetation which grows in a particular place depends on both the landform of the area and the climate.

The **pie graph** opposite shows the **proportions** of the different types of vegetation in Papua New Guinea. It shows us that nearly three-quarters (75 per cent) of Papua New Guinea is covered by **forest**.

Grassland
Savanna
Swamp
Tropical forest
Mangrove

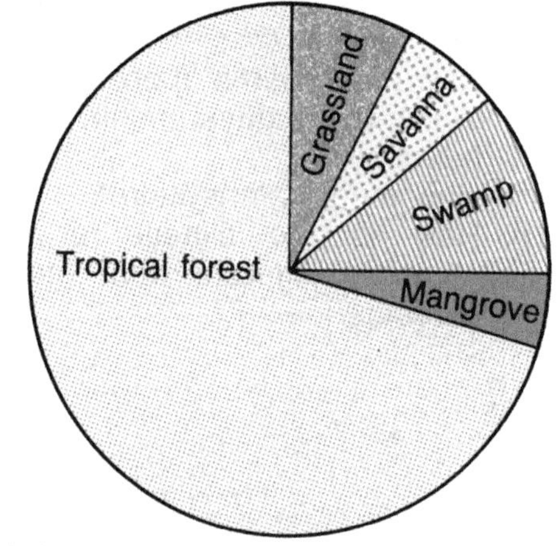

Relative amounts of vegetation types in Papua New Guinea.

Vegetation and Landforms

Compare the vegetation map (page 30) with the landforms map (page 11). If we study the two maps carefully we can see some similar patterns. For example:

- **mangrove vegetation** is found only in coastal lowlands
- **swamp vegetation** is found in lowland areas, particularly in river valleys such as the Fly and the Sepik
- **forest** is found in both lowland areas and highland areas
- **grassland** is found mainly in areas of very high land.

Rainforest.

Vegetation and Climate

Now compare the vegetation map (page 30) with the climate map (page 23).

Again, similar patterns can be seen, for example:

- **mangroves, swamp vegetation** and **forests** all grow in hot, wet, climates
- **grassland** is associated with cool, mountain climates
- **savanna** is found **only** where there is a distinct dry season.

Mangroves.

Swamp.

Mountain grassland.

Savanna vegetation near Port Moresby.

Vegetation and Mountains

In Chapter 3 we learned that the higher we go up a mountain the cooler it gets. This has a very big effect on the forests that grow there.

Not long ago a group of schoolboys walked over the famous Kokoda Trail. Their account of the journey describes very well the changes in climate and vegetation they saw as they travelled from the lowlands of Oro Province, across the high Central Ranges, to the lowlands of Central Province.

A Walk over the Kokoda Trail

We left Kokoda on a hot, sunny morning. The first two hours of walking took us through the flat land of the Kokoda rubber plantation. The trees were widely and neatly spaced, and everywhere we could see labourers tapping the trees for their sap which would soon be turned into rubber. After the plantation we entered a cool and green forest of evergreen trees.

Lower mountain forest.

Lowland rainforest.

The trees were very tall and the leaves at the top were so close together that very little light reached the forest floor. We were walking on a carpet of dead leaves, twigs, and old branches. The smell of rotting vegetation was very strong.

The trail climbed upwards through the forest as we made our way towards the crest of the first ridge. When we got to the first crest there was a short downhill walk before the next ridge loomed ahead of us. As we climbed higher, we noticed that the forest vegetation was changing.

Here we began to see pine trees growing amongst the evergreens. The forest was drier and not as dark as the lowland forest. Many people live in this area and there were large patches of kunai grass growing where the forest had been cleared to make gardens.

After midday on the second day of walking we reached the highest point on the trail. This was Mount Bellamy, 2300 metres above sea level. Here it was very cool and the hilltops were often covered in mist.

This part of the forest was very cold and wet. The trees were often covered by mist and water dripped everywhere. Because of the cold and dampness, the trees are smaller here and covered with masses of grey, damp moss. The forest was quiet, with only the sound of dripping water and our squelching footsteps to break the silence. Some of us felt quite scared.

For the next two days we walked up and down countless ridges and valleys. We waded across many fast-flowing mountain streams making their rapid way down to the lowlands. The valleys here are well populated. The people make their gardens on the sides of the valleys where they have cleared the forest. These people are mainly subsistence farmers, which means that they grow all their own food, but they do sell oranges, bananas, and green vegetables to people who walk over the trail.

The Sogeri Plateau.

Moss forest.

After the valleys we once again descended to the lowland rainforest. Two more days walking, and we finally descended Imita Ridge, arriving at Owers Corner on the Sogeri Plateau, 600 metres above sea level. The forests here were cut down long ago to grow rubber trees. Now, the rubber is being cut down and cattle graze on the grassland that grows instead. A 45 minute PMV ride later we were all back at sea level in Port Moresby.

We were all very tired from our long walk and we slept very deeply that night. However, we will never forget the interesting things that we saw on our journey, nor the people who helped us on our way.

Summary of Main Ideas

Papua New Guinea has five main types of vegetation:

- forest
- grassland
- savanna
- swamp
- mangrove.

The vegetation is influenced by **climate** and **landforms**.

People have cleared areas of natural vegetation to allow them to use the land for:

- gardening
- plantations
- cattle.

Activities

Exercises

1. Fill in the missing words in the paragraph below. You will need to look back in the chapter to find the missing words.

   All the plants that are found in an area make up the ________ of that place. ________ **rainforest** is the most common type of rainforest in Papua New Guinea. Large areas of ______ are found in the lowland valleys of the Sepik, Markham, and Ramu rivers. Where water is unable to drain away very easily, _____ are formed. Some parts of the country have a long dry season and because of this ________ woodland is the only vegetation that can grow there.

2. Label the following diagram of a rainforest:

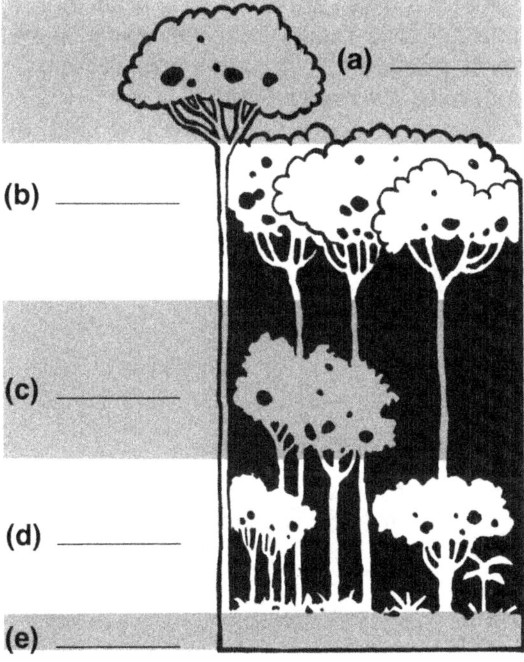

Things to Discuss

1. Why is the rainforest floor covered with dead leaves and not much new growth? (Remember that the leaves do not let much sunlight through.)
2. What natural vegetation exists around your area? List some of the uses that people make of the vegetation.
3. What vegetation has been planted by people in your area? What is this vegetation used for?
4. Has the removal of any vegetation in your area caused any problems, such as hard soil or cracks in the ground?
5. What can be done to stop the forests from disappearing altogether? Why is this important?
6. One result of making gardens is that grassland replaces the natural forest. This can be a good thing and this can be a bad thing. Discuss what the good and bad things are and make a list in your book.

Things to Do

1. Take a walk through the countryside in your area. Describe the landforms and vegetation that you see.
2. On an outline map of Papua New Guinea, mark in the names of the places mentioned in this chapter. Using a key, mark in the main vegetation regions. Page 23 of the Papua New Guinea School Atlas will help you.

5. The Human Environment: Land Use

Changes to the Land

People use the land for many things. People **change** the natural environment when they use the land.

Look at the following examples and see how people have changed the natural environment.

Subsistence Garden

A small area of land has been cleared and crops are being grown.

In about three years the garden will be abandoned and the natural vegetation will grow back again.

This is a **small** change to the natural environment.

Subsistence garden.

Plantation agriculture: a large change in the environment.

Plantation Agriculture

Here a **large** area of land has been cleared and many coconut trees have been planted. This plantation will grow coconuts for many years.

This is a **large** change in the natural environment.

Logging

Here the natural vegetation (the tall forest trees) is being cut down and carried away to be sold.

Logging.

Large-scale Mining Operation

Valuable minerals are found in some rocks in the ground, e.g. gold, copper. To obtain the minerals for sale people have to cut away the surface of the earth. This changes the natural environment a lot.

A large-scale mining operation.

Rural Town

Here the natural environment has been changed in many ways. Trade stores have been built to sell goods. Roads have been built for people to travel on. Houses have been built for town workers to live in.

A rural town.

Port Moresby

Port Moresby is the largest city in Papua New Guinea. The natural environment is almost completely hidden by things people have made.

Port Moresby.

Oala Oala Rarua Beach Reserve

This photograph shows land used for tourism. The natural environment is not changed very much. Most tourists travel to our country to see the natural environment.

Oala Oala Rarua beach reserve, N.C.D.

Land Use in Papua New Guinea

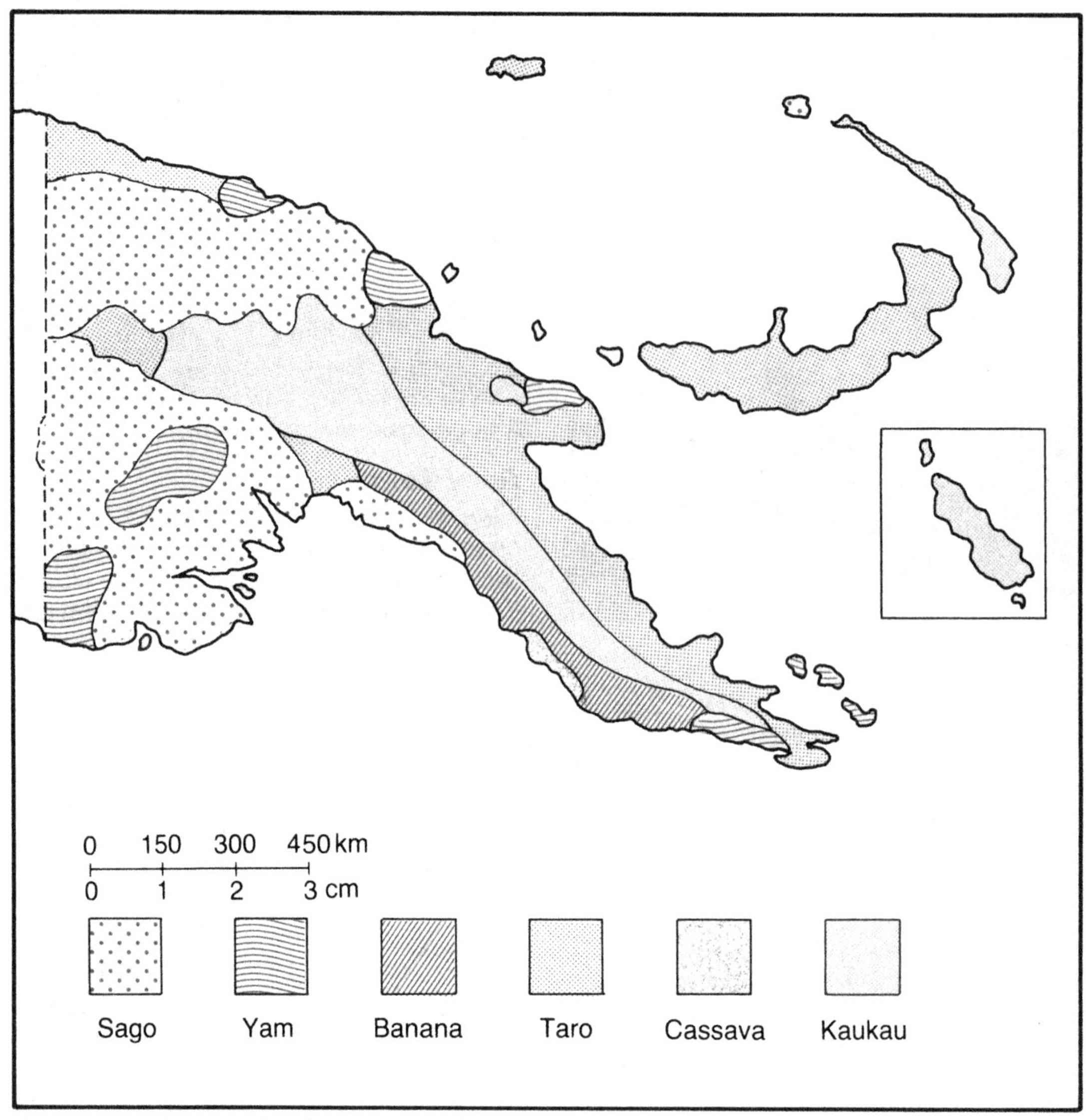

Subsistence farming (main crop areas).

The map above shows the areas where one food crop is the main source of food. The main food of a group of people is called the **staple** food. Most of the land use of our country is **subsistence farming**. Subsistence farming, or growing your own food, does not change the natural environment very much.

All the other types of land use are for **commercial activities**. This means that people make money from the way they use the land. Places where there is commercial land use are shown in the map on the next page.

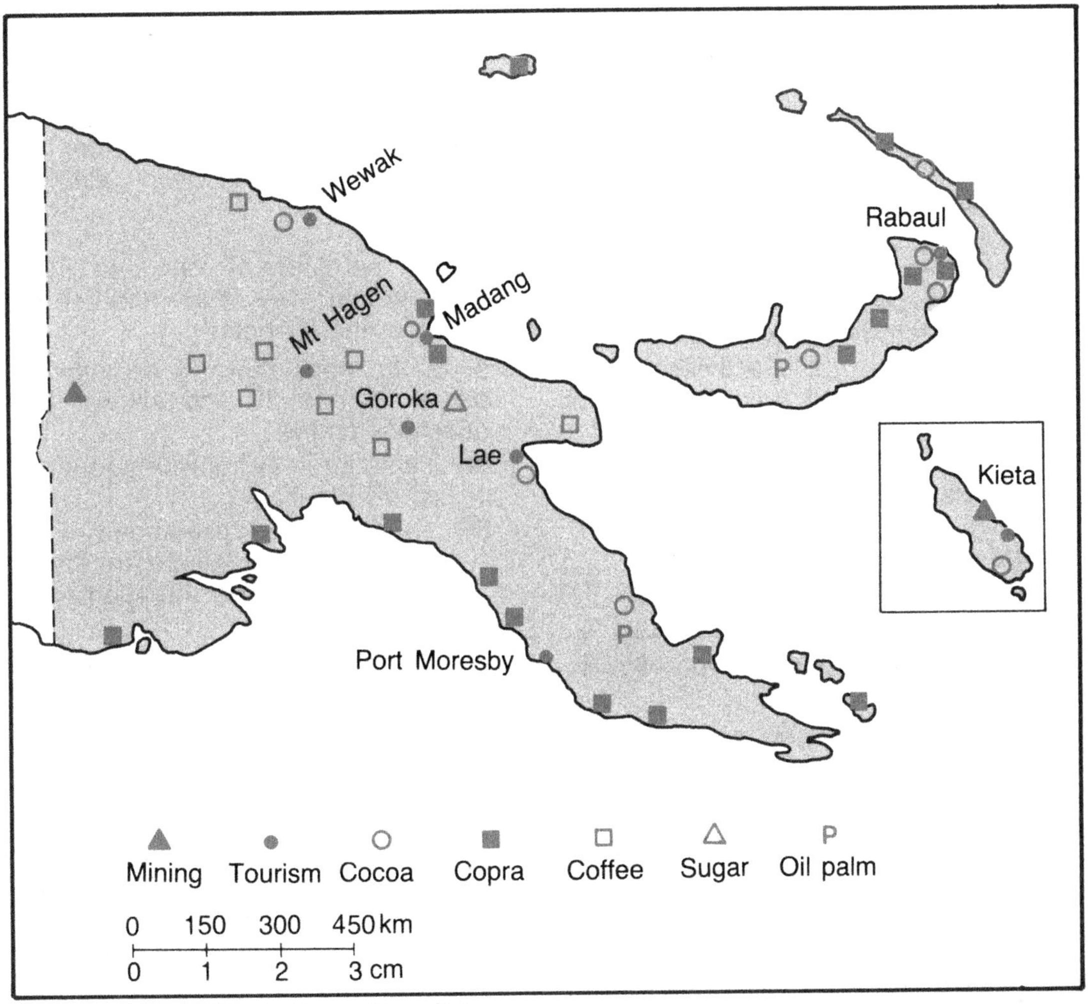

Commercial activities in Papua New Guinea.

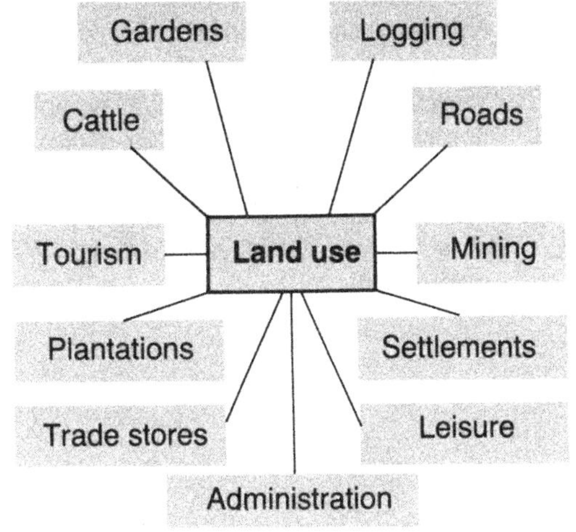

Types of land use in Papua New Guinea.

Summary of Main Ideas

The human environment is that part of the natural environment that people have changed.

Subsistence gardening is the most widespread form of land use in Papua New Guinea.

Most land use (except for subsistence gardening) is for **commercial** (money-making) purposes.

Activities

Exercises

1. Fill in the missing words in the paragraph below:

   The way the land is used is part of the ________ environment. ________ farming is the type of land use in which people grow crops for themselves. Activities that make money are called ________ activities. The food that makes up most of a person's diet is called the ________ food. The main food crop of swampy areas is ________.

Things to Discuss

1. What is the human environment?
2. What have the people done to change the natural environment in your area? Make a list.
3. How is the land used in your area? Make a list.

Things to Do

1. Draw the following table in your book.

Part of the Natural Environment	Part of the Human Environment

   Put the following words under the correct heading in the table.

   town canoe tree liana path garden dam river rain sunshine cattle tobacco tuna oil palm

2. Talk to the elders of your area. Find out how their way of life and use of the land has changed.
3. Study the maps showing land use on pages 38 and 39 and answer the questions below.
   (a) Name three towns where tourism is important.
   (b) Name three provinces that produce copra. Where are these areas located, in the Highlands or on islands?
   (c) Name one place where sugar is grown commercially. What type of landform area is it?
   (d) Where is most of the coffee grown in Papua New Guinea?
   (e) What is the staple food of people living in the Highlands?
   (f) Find out the names of the two places marked on the map where there are large-scale oil palm projects.
   (g) In what part of the country is taro the main subsistence crop?
   (h) Name one province where the yam is the main food.
   (i) What is the staple food of people living in the lowland river valleys of the Fly and the Sepik?
   (j) Name the two areas marked on the map where mining is important.

6. The Human Environment: Settlement

Houses

People build houses wherever they live. Protection from the weather is an important reason for living in a house. In Chapter 3 you learned that the climate of a place can tell you what type of weather to expect. This also affects the type of houses that people build.

A Highland round house.

A Highland Round House

There are no windows in this house. This is to keep the house **warm** during the cold Highland nights.

Remember that Highland climates are colder than lowland climates.

A Lowland Stilt House

This house has many windows. This is to keep the house **cool** in the hot lowland climate. The stilts also help to keep the house cool by allowing air to move underneath the house. They also help to protect the house from floods.

A lowland stilt house.

Villages

People usually live together in groups. A small group of houses is called a **village**.

Villages usually have a few houses, a food store, a church, and a place where the whole community can gather. They are found mainly in areas where people use the land for growing crops. These are called **rural** areas.

Each dot on this map is a village. The map shows that there can be many small villages in one area. Notice that many of these villages are close to the road.

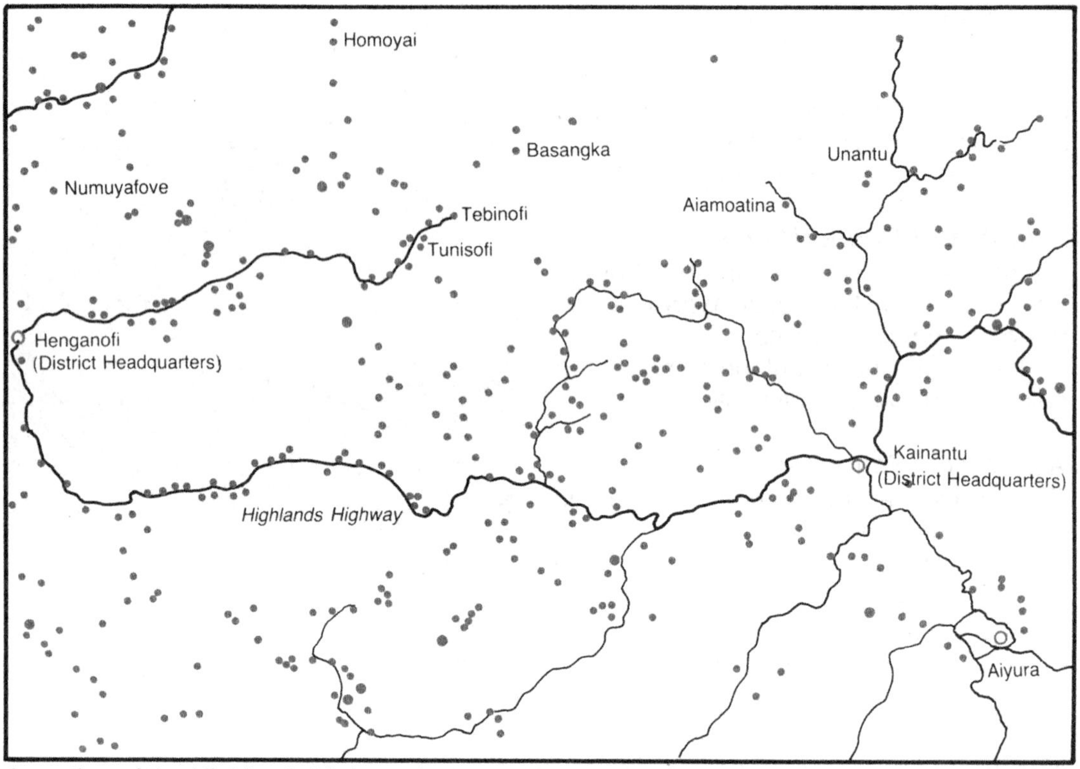

A section of the Highlands Highway between Kainantu and Henganofi. Each dot on this map is a village.

Geographers are often interested in the pattern of houses in a village. They study **settlement patterns**.

Village Houses in a Line

The houses in this photograph are quite close together, but they are all built along the road in a line.

This is a **linear** pattern of houses.

All the houses here are near to the road.

Village houses in a line.

Village Houses in a Group

Villages that are not found close to roads (e.g. villages on a hilltop) often have houses close together in a circular group.

This settlement has a **circular** pattern.

One reason for this pattern is to protect all the houses from attack by an enemy tribe.

Before colonial government, houses in South Bougainville were in the circular pattern. After colonial government, the local administrators, the **luluais**, forced the villagers to build their houses in a linear pattern. The luluais thought this made the villages easier to govern.

Village houses in a group.

Towns and Cities

When large numbers of people live together, settlement patterns become more complicated. Shops and offices are built, and people go there to work. In this way, a village becomes a **town**. A town has buildings for more purposes than a village.

Towns can grow even bigger, especially if there is a good reason for people to go there. For example, there may be a good harbour, as at Rabaul. If a town becomes a provincial centre, it will contain the administrative buildings for the Province and it will also grow bigger.

Port Moresby is our largest city.

A rural town.

Areas where many people live together in large settlements, and where most of the space is taken up with houses and other buildings, are called **urban** areas.

Very large towns are called **cities**. The city where the centre of government is located is called the **capital city**. Port Moresby is the capital city of Papua New Guinea.

In Papua New Guinea, only 15 per cent of the people live in towns and cities. This means that our country is mainly rural.

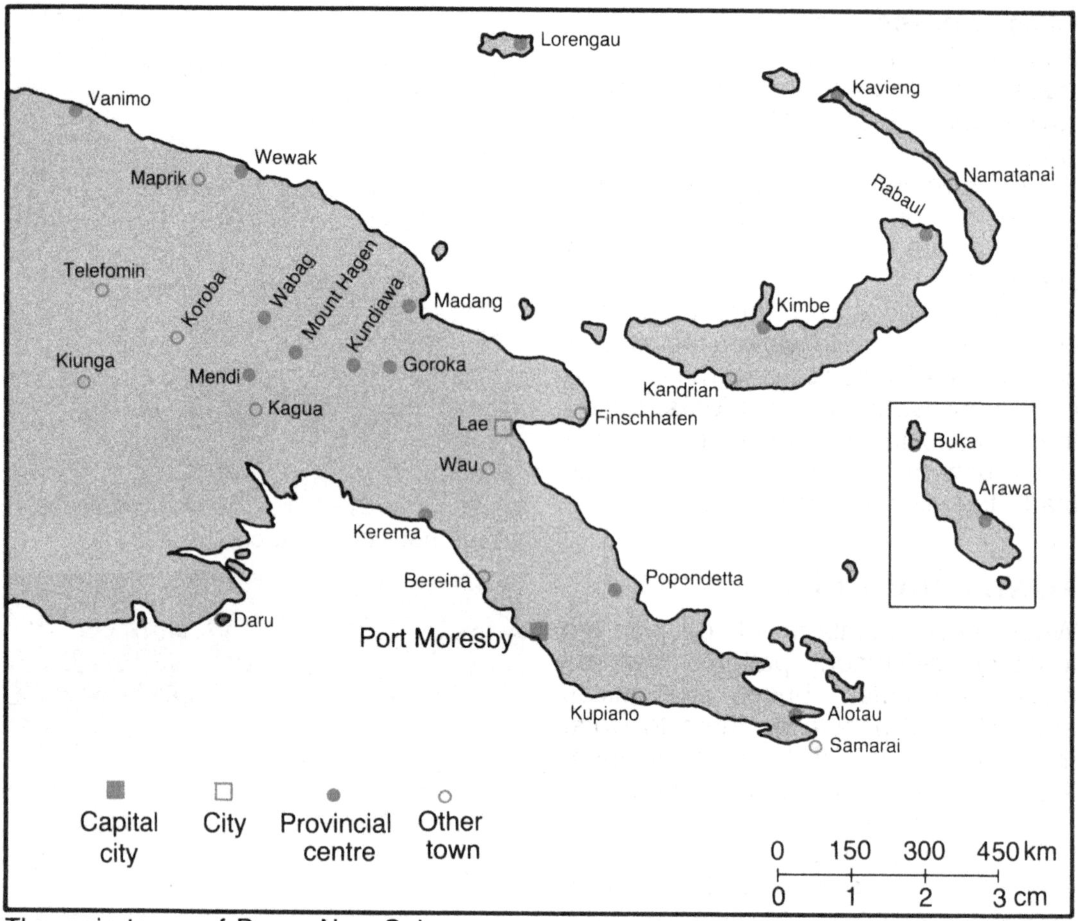

The main towns of Papua New Guinea.

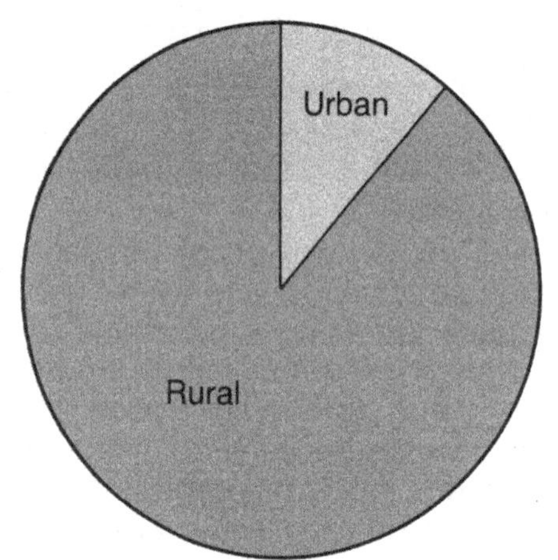

The relative proportions of urban and rural population in Papua New Guinea.

Summary of Main Ideas

There are many different types of settlement in Papua New Guinea.

The two main types of settlement are **rural** and **urban**.

Most of the people of Papua New Guinea live in the **rural** areas.

Activities

Exercises

1. Fill in the blanks in the following paragraph.

   A ________ is usually a small group of houses with a church and a community gathering place. A ________ consists of a larger group of buildings. The buildings in a town are usually for more ________ than those in a village. Provincial centres contain the ________ buildings for the whole province. The ________ ________ contains the centre of government for the whole country.

2. Write a list of all the provinces in Papua New Guinea. Next to each province write the name of the administrative centre.
3. Look at the map of towns in Papua New Guinea on page 44. Use the scale to find out how far it is from:
   (a) Rabaul to Lae
   (b) Vanimo to Alotau
   (c) Mendi to Goroka
   (d) Kavieng to Daru.
4. Use the direction pointer on the same map to find out the direction of:
   (a) Port Moresby **from** Popondetta
   (b) Kieta **from** Wewak
   (c) Madang **from** Kerema
   (d) Mount Hagen **from** Lorengau.

Things to Discuss

1. How have the houses been arranged in your area? Why?
2. Why do settlements get more complicated as they get bigger?

Things to Do

1. Visit your nearest town. Is it urban or rural? Make a list of the different purposes of the buildings.
2. Draw a map showing the pattern of buildings in your school. Include a key and a scale.

7. The Human Environment: Transport

In Chapter 5 you learned that, in Papua New Guinea, people use the land to produce many things, such as minerals and crops. Papua New Guinea sells many of these things to other countries. **Transport** is needed to move things from place to place.

Transport in Papua New Guinea.

Road Transport

Road transport in our country is very difficult. This is because Papua New Guinea is very mountainous and thick forests cover most of the land. It is very expensive to build the roads, but once the roads have been built, road transport is very cheap.

There are about 800 kilometres of **sealed** road in Papua New Guinea. Most of the sealed roads are found in and around the provincial centres. The longest sealed road is the Highlands Highway which runs from Lae to Tomba in Western Highlands Province.

There are many more kilometres of **unsealed** road than there are of sealed road. One problem of unsealed roads is that they are easily eroded by the heavy rainfall.

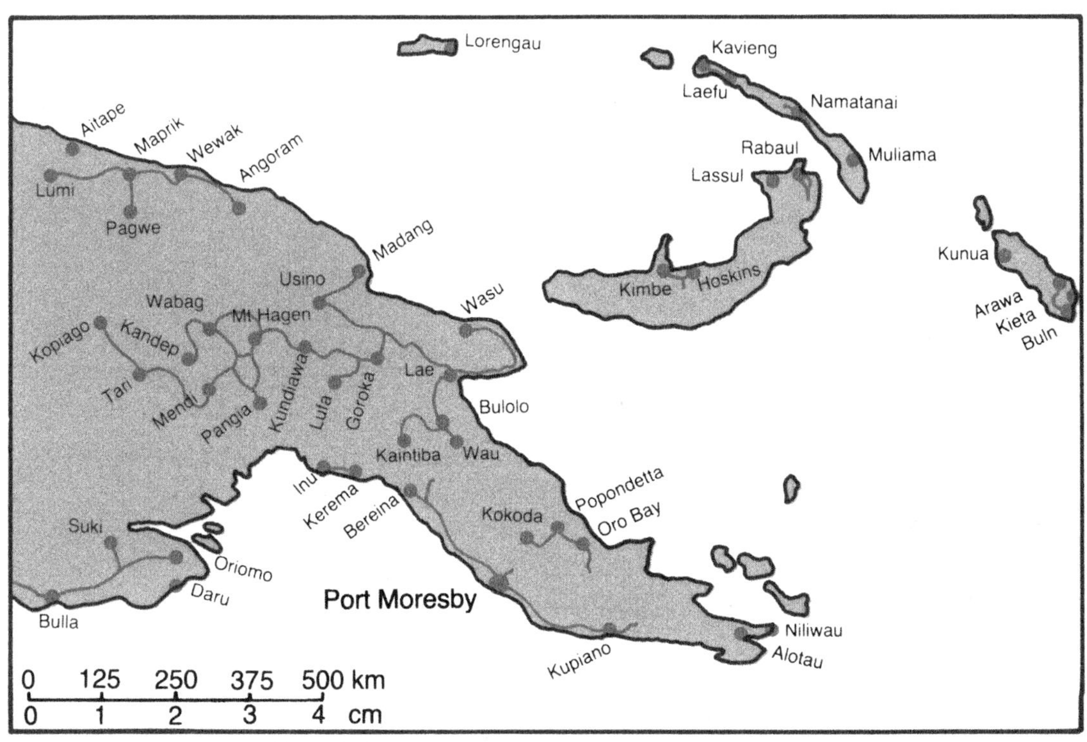

Main roads of Papua New Guinea.

Air Transport

Air transport is very important to the development of our country because it is so difficult to build roads to link all the provincial centres.

Air transport is very expensive because there is only a small amount of space available to carry cargo on the aeroplanes.

Sea Transport

Products such as copra, cocoa, timber, and minerals are heavy and take up a lot of space, so they are transported by sea. Sea transport is the cheapest form of transport, although it is usually the slowest as well.

Ships from overseas come to most of our major ports. Goods that are sold to overseas countries are called **exports**. Goods bought from overseas are called **imports**.

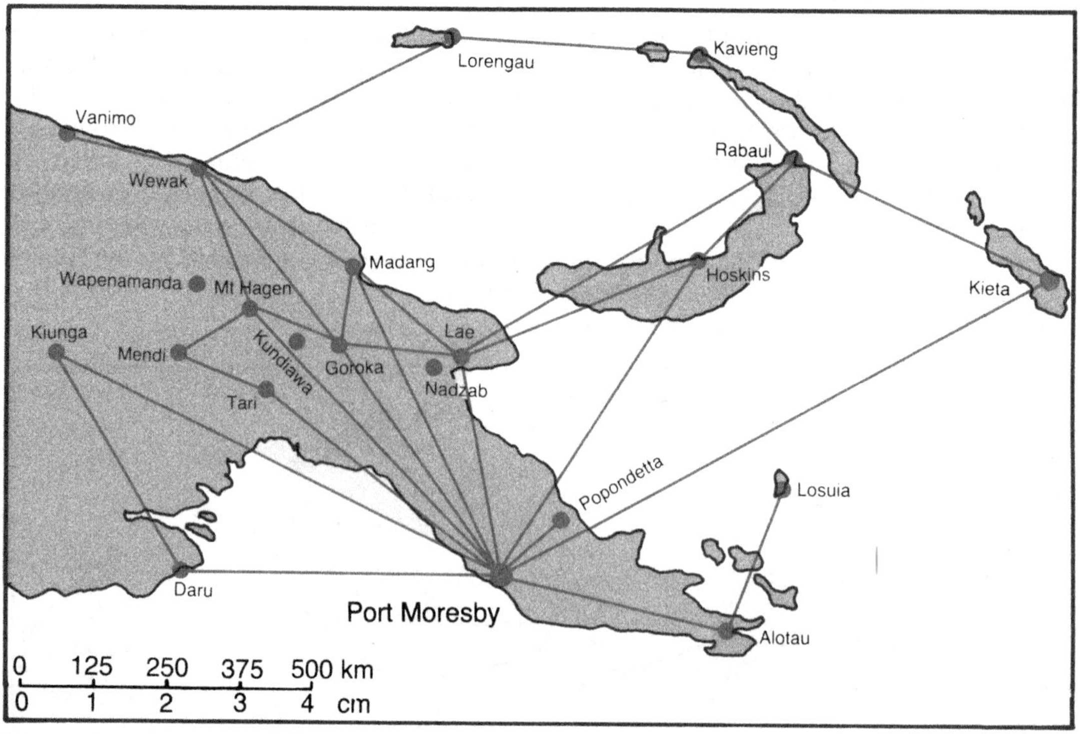

The major air routes of Papua New Guinea.

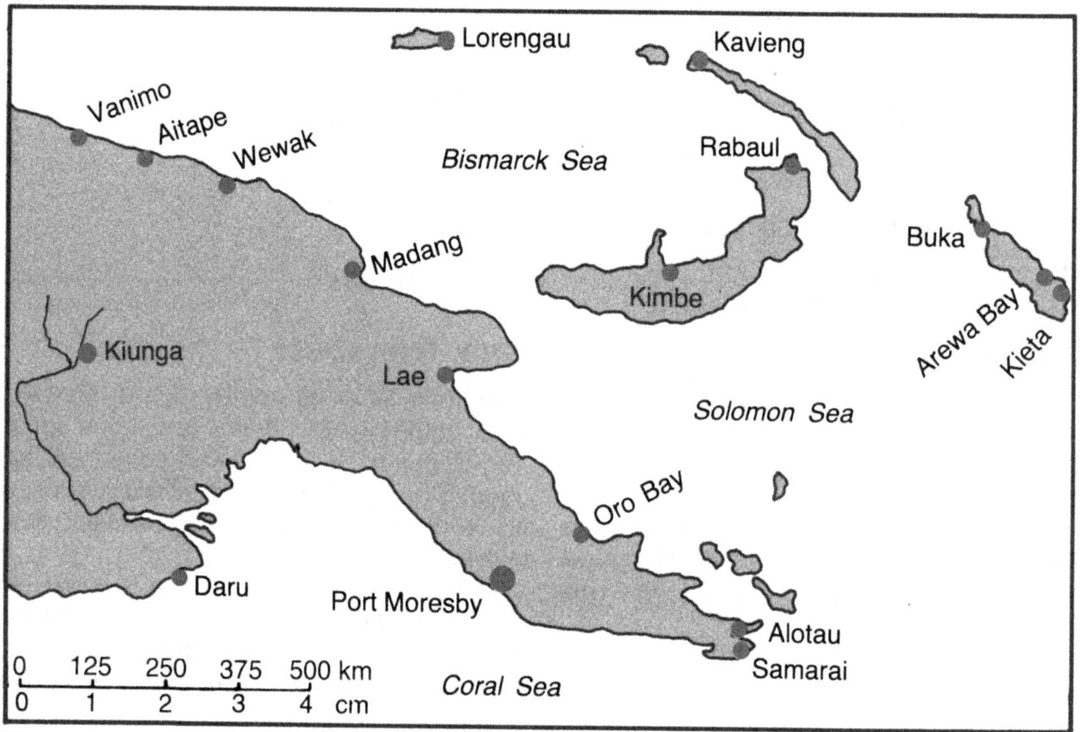

The major ports of Papua New Guinea.

Pokol's Journey

Many people can now travel all over the country. Follow this journey made by Pokol from Gerehu in Port Moresby to his village 10 kilometres from Agaun in Milne Bay Province. His village is in a rural area and is not near a main road or airport. Pokol's village is **isolated**. Pokol uses many different forms of transport so that he can visit his brother for Christmas.

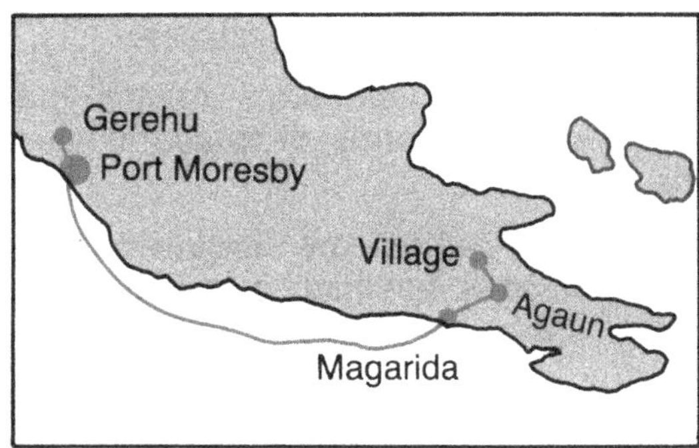

Map of Pokol's journey.

1. Gerehu to Port Moresby.

Pokol has to take 2 PMVs to get to the wharf from Gerehu.
Time: 1½ hours
Cost: 60 toea
Distance: 8 km

2. Port Moresby to Magarida.

The boat to Magarida follows the coast. Pokol sees many dolphins.
Time: 36 hours
Cost: K20
Distance: 270 km

3. Magarida to Agaun.

Pokol travels by third level airline over mountainous country.
Time: 10 minutes
Cost: K30
Distance: 30 km

4. Agaun to Pokol's village.

Pokol travels by foot through thick forest and over many streams.
Time: 8 hours
Cost: nothing
Distance: 10 km

Summary of Main Ideas

The variety of landforms means that many different forms of transport must be used.

Most rural areas are **isolated** from urban centres because of the difficulty of transport.

Air transport is expensive but is necessary to link areas separated by mountains and seas.

Road transport is a cheap form of transport but is very limited due to the mountainous country and the thick forests.

Sea transport is also cheap, but it is slow. It is mainly used to carry large amounts of heavy products.

Activities

Exercises

1. Fill in the blanks in the following paragraph.

   ________ transport is difficult in Papua New Guinea because of the thick forest and high mountains. The heavy rainfall often erodes ________ roads. Air transport is very ________ because the space for cargo is ________. Sea transport is used mainly for carrying ________ amounts of cargo. Goods that are sent overseas are called ________.

2. Which form of transport is best for the following purposes?
   (a) Copper concentrate from Bougainville to Australia
   (b) Coffee beans from the Highlands to Lae
   (c) Vegetables from the Highlands to Port Moresby
   (d) Coconuts from the plantation to the copra processing centre
   (e) People from Australia to Papua New Guinea
   (f) Letters from Port Moresby to Rabaul.

Things to Discuss

1. Discuss your answers to Exercise 2 above. Can more than one type of transport be used in each case? Which is the best type of transport and why?

2. Why is transport so important to the development of Papua New Guinea?

Things to Do

1. Make a survey of the types of transport in your area. Find out how many people use the following types of transport.

   (a) walking
   (b) car
   (c) aeroplane
   (d) ship.

2. Collect pictures of different types of transport used in Papua New Guinea. What is each one used for? Make a chart to show the different uses of transport in Papua New Guinea.

8. A Case Study: The Abelam People

In this book you have learned many things about the natural and human environments. The natural environment influences the way people live. Also, people can change the natural environment and make it part of the human environment.

In this chapter you will learn about the Abelam people of East Sepik Province. You will learn how they **interact** with their environment.

Location

The Abelam people live in the north of East Sepik Province. Maprik is the nearest town. The plains and grasslands of the mighty Sepik River are to the south.

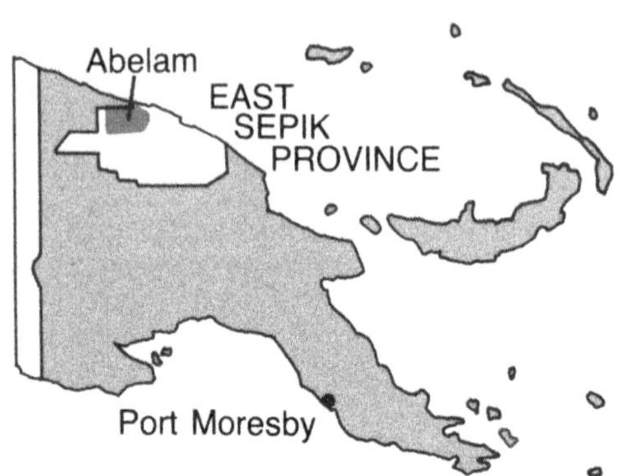

The location of the Abelam people.

The Natural Environment

The Abelam people live in the Torricelli Ranges which separate the Sepik River valley from the north coast. This is a mountainous region with many narrow valleys. The villages of the Abelam people are built on the sides of the mountains. The vegetation surrounding the villages is rainforest.

Temperatures are high all the year round. Rain falls all the year round but there is a less wet (**dry**) season from May to September.

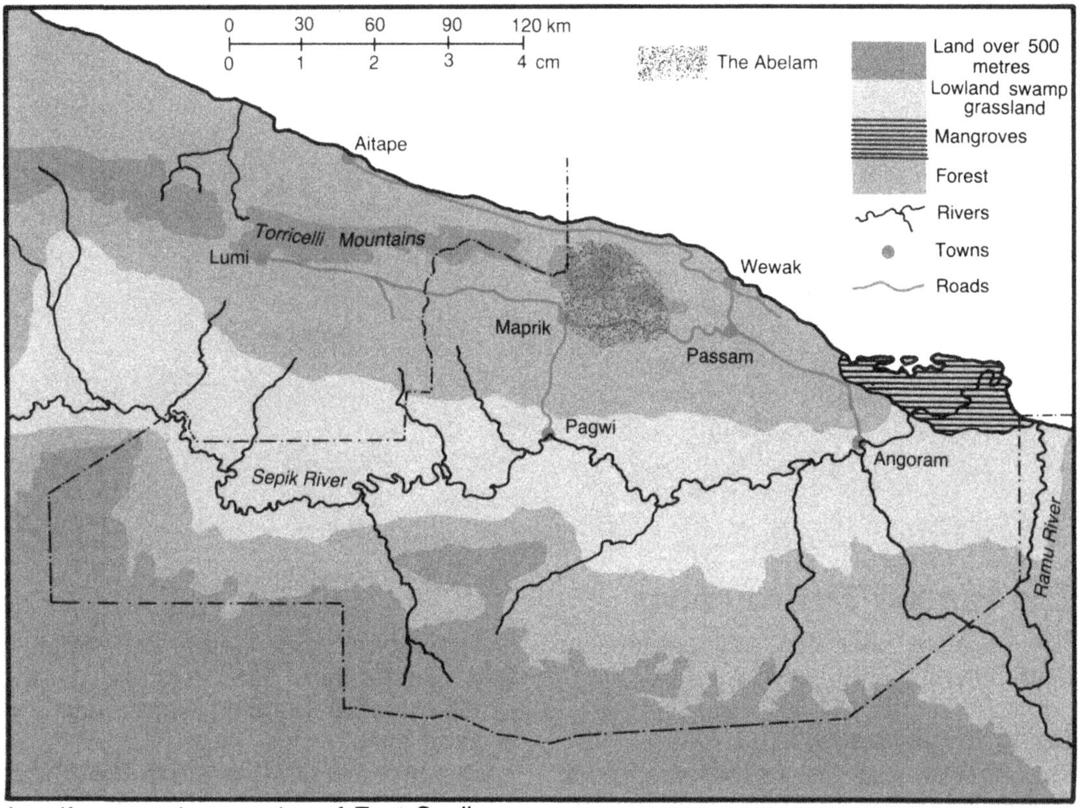

Landforms and vegetation of East Sepik Province.

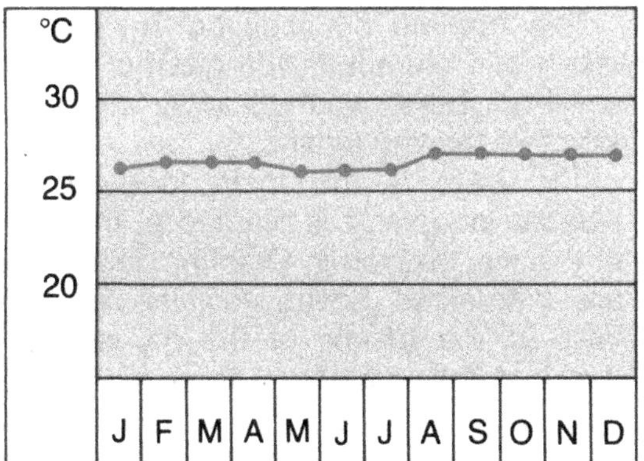

Average monthly temperatures.

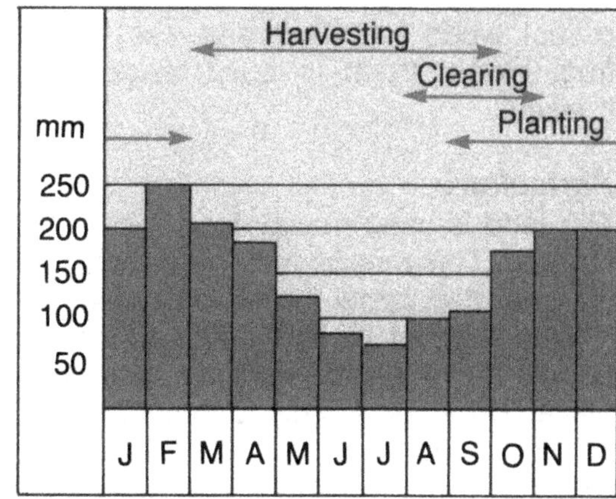

Average monthly rainfall.

The Abelam environment.

The Human Environment

The Abelam use the environment in many ways.

Using the Rainforest

The Abelam use the natural resources of the rainforest to meet their needs. They gather fruit and nuts to eat, they collect wood for fires, and use timber from bigger trees to build fences and houses.

Agriculture

The land is used mainly for subsistence farming. This means that the people rely on what they grow for all their food.

When a plot of land is used up the people leave it and move on to another place. They come back to that land after several years when the soil has regained its fertility. This is called **shifting cultivation**.

They clear their gardens in August and September. The woman in the photograph is planting yams using a digging stick.

Because the land is steep they have to be careful that the soil is not washed away by the rain. The washing away of soil by rain is called **erosion**.

The Abelam put logs on the ground and leave stumps in the ground to stop soil from being washed away down the sides of the mountains.

The yam is the main food of the Abelam people. It is planted at the start of the wet season in October. The yams are harvested seven to nine months later in the middle of the dry season. (Look at the rainfall graph on page 53.) It is very important for the people to arrange their farming activities to suit the climate.

An Abelam garden.

Understanding Nature

The Abelam way of life is very closely linked to the natural environment. The people need to understand the climate, landforms, and natural vegetation to survive.

When the Abelam choose the plot for a garden they look closely at the vegetation. If the leaves of the trees are light green it means that the land has not rested enough since it was last used. They also study the wild animals and insects there. If there are white ants in the soil, it means that the land is not ready for planting.

Changing the Natural Environment

The Abelam live in close co-operation with nature. They also make small changes to their environment. When they plant gardens they clear the forest. They also build houses and villages with paths and roads to link them together.

Settlement

The Abelam people build large villages made up of small groups of houses. Each group has about four sleeping houses, four storage huts, two cooking houses, a few shelter houses, pig houses, and latrines (toilets). Each village has between ten and thirty of these groups. This means that the villages are spread out over a large area on the mountain slopes.

Work

The people changed from a purely subsistence life-style long ago. They now grow coffee as a cash crop. This means that the land is used more and more often. When land is used like this we say that the activity is **intensive**. A good transport system is needed to move their coffee to the Coffee Marketing Board. Yams can be stored for a long time but coffee cannot. The transport system must therefore be reliable.

The nearest town is Maprik. From Maprik there is a good road to Wewak. There is also an air service which links Maprik and Wewak. Wewak has good port facilities to export the coffee.

Population

The Abelam population is growing. Many more people are now living in the villages. This is mainly due to better health services and medicines. This bigger population can bring new problems. More food must be grown so more of the land is used for gardens. Sometimes there is no extra land for gardening and so the same gardens are used more often. The soil does not get as long to rest and the crops do not produce as much food as before. The rainforest does not get a chance to grow back and so may be permanently changed.

Summary of Main Ideas

Shifting cultivation and **subsistence agriculture** are the traditional farming methods of people living in the rainforest.

People live by using the natural environment to supply their needs.

Nowadays more people are growing **cash crops** to earn money to help supply their needs.

Land use is **intensive** if the same land is used year after year to produce as much as possible.

If too much is taken from the natural environment then the environment may become permanently changed.

The study of geography involves *describing* the *natural* and the *human environments*. It also involves the study of how people *interact* with their environment.

Activities

Exercises

Fill in the blanks.

1. The tropical lowland rainforest can be a ________ for people.
2. In traditional life-styles, people were ________ gardeners.
3. ________ cultivation is done by moving from plot to plot.
4. Commercial activities are more ____ than subsistence activities.
5. The Abelam live in the ________ Mountains.
6. The word to describe the washing away of soil is ________.
7. The staple food grown by the Abelam is the ________.

Things to Discuss

1. What do you understand by a traditional life-style?
2. Why are traditional life-styles in Papua New Guinea changing?
3. Why do you think it is important to shift garden plots in shifting cultivation?
4. How do people change the land?
5. Discuss the effects of climate on the Abelam. (Hint: look at the questions in Chapter 3.)
6. What problems do too many people cause? How would you solve the problem of too many people?

Things to Do

1. Find out from your family or from the elders in your area how they gardened when they were young. Draw a diagram to show this.
2. Pretend you are a traditional shifting farmer. Act out the stages of shifting cultivation.
3. Complete the following chart using information from this chapter.

The Life-style of the Abelam	
Natural Environment	**Description**
(a) Location **(b)** Climate **(c)** Landforms **(d)** Vegetation	
Human Environment	**Description**
(a) Gardening **(b)** Settlement **(c)** People	

Glossary

Word	Page	Meaning
alluvium	17	fine particles of soil dropped by rivers.
altitude	24	height above sea level usually measured in metres.
Antarctic circle	5	the line of latitude close to the south pole.
Arctic circle	5	the line of latitude close to the north pole.
cash crops	55	crops grown to sell to make money.
circular	42	round like a circle.
climate	21	the pattern of rainfall and temperature over a long period of time.
commercial activities	37	activities that make money.
continents	5	the land that makes up the earth.
coral	16	the hard substance built on the sea bed by small sea creatures.
deposition	17	the material that has been left or dropped by the river.
drought	25	not enough water to grow crops.
earth's crust	13	soil and hard rock, several kilometres thick, which make up the earth's surface.
earthquake	15	a sudden movement of the earth's surface.
environment	1	natural and human surroundings.
Equator	5	the line that is drawn around the middle of the globe.
equivalent to	2	standing for.
erosion	17	the wearing away of land, by water, wind and ice.
eruption	15	when the melted rock comes up through the surface of the earth.
exports	46	goods that are sold to overseas countries.
fault	14	a crack in the layers of rock caused by movements of the earth's crust.
fold	13	a bend in the layers of rock caused by the movements of the earth's crust.
frost	25	the ground becomes frozen during the coldest part of the night.
geographer	1	person who studies the earth and all the things on it.
geography	1	the study of the earth and all the things on it.
human environment	1	everything in the surroundings that people have changed or made.
ice caps	5	the areas around the south and north poles that are covered by ice all the year round.
imports	46	goods that are bought from overseas countries.
intensive farming	55	carrying out a lot of farming activities on a small area of land.
interact	51	act with each other.
isolated	49	far away from the main area.
key	2	a list of symbols used on a map.
landforms	11	the shape of the land e.g. highlands, lowlands, valleys.
linear	41	in a straight line.
lines of latitude	5	the lines that are drawn on the globe that run from east to west.

Word	Page	Meaning
location	2	where a place or thing is.
lowlands	11	the flat area close to the coast.
map	2	a way of representing the earth's surface on a flat piece of paper.
mist	33	clouds at or near the earth's surface.
natural environment	1	everything in the surroundings made by nature e.g. trees, rivers, mountains.
natural hazards	25	dangerous natural events e.g. cyclones, volcanic eruptions, floods.
northern hemisphere	5	the northern half of the globe.
ocean	7	the water that surrounds the continents.
plantation agriculture	35	large areas of land planted with cash crops e.g. coffee, sugarcane, tea.
rainfall	20	the total amount of rain falling on a given area during a particular time.
rainforest	34	jungle; thick tropical forest.
resources	53	things that are useful to people.
rural	36	area where most of the land is used for growing crops.
savanna	31	a large area of grassland with a few trees.
settlement	41	a place where people have built houses to live permanently e.g. village and town.
shifting cultivation	53	type of farming in which the plot of land being cultivated is changed from time to time.
soil	18	top layer of the earth's crust.
southern hemisphere	5	the southern half of the globe.
staple food	37	the main daily food eaten by a group of people.
subsistence farming	35	type of farming in which the produce is used mainly by the farmer and his family.
swamp	18	an area of land which is always wet and which is usually overgrown with vegetation.
symbol	2	sign or shape which is used to represent something.
temperate countries	5	countries located between the two polar circles and the tropics.
temperature	20	how hot or cold a place is.
temperature range	29	the difference between the highest temperature and the lowest temperature.
Tropic of Cancer	5	the line of latitude drawn on the northern side of the equator.
Tropic of Capricorn	5	the line of latitude drawn on the southern side of the equator.
tropical climate	23	hot and wet all year round.
tropics	5	the lines of latitude drawn on either side of the equator.
urban area	42	area where many people live together in large settlements.
valley	12	the land between mountains or hills.
vegetation	1	plants and trees growing in an area.
volcano	15	hill or mountain through which gases, lava and ashes come up from below the earth's crust.
weather	20	the day to day amounts of rainfall, cloud, sunshine, wind and temperature.

Index